COME And DINE

WITH THE

KING

Your Personal Invitation

By Elaine C. Rumley

SHININ
LIGHT PUBLICATIONS

Shining Light Publications
P.O. Box 836023
Richardson, TX 75083

www.xulonpress.com

To: Pastor Norma—

May the Lord inspire and
strengthen you through these
pages— You are indeed a
Worthy Warrior!

Love + appreciate you
Elaine
Rev.
July 5, 2014

Acknowledgements

My personal thanks to all the friends and intercessors

who took the time to encourage me along this writing journey.

The many who prayed and kept asking if the book was done.

This book is truly a miracle of His grace—cover to cover!

I pray these pages work a "miracle" in your life too!

My special thanks to Amalia Villarreal, Yolanda Obaze

and Carolyn Sue Daniels for the many hours

in researching, editing and checking the details.

I thank graphic designer Okebaram Ekwuribe

for his dedication in finishing the cover designs.

With a grateful heart, I thank the Lord

for His faithfulness, love and continual inspiration.

He is indeed the *life giver*!

This book and my life are forever dedicated to Him.

Elaine Rumley

Introduction

Altar: A place dedicated and set aside for the purpose of meeting with God.

That definition is a simplification for a modern context in today's church.

In Hebrew the word altar was **mizbeah**, which has a root meaning of "slaughter," defining it as a location for animal sacrifice for sin offerings. The Greek of the New Testament is **thusiasterion**, "a place of sacrifice." Whether the context is the sacrificial system of the Old Testament or a place of honor within the New Testament, the altar is a place of remembrance and still a place of dedication to meet with and honor God.

The heartbeat written through the pages of this book is from an author who has lived this principle all her life. I remember growing up as a child and my mom finding a way to have her "war room;" a place set aside in our house for prayer and time with God.

Among the maps, missionaries, prayer needs and scriptures, I remember my picture, report cards, and girl friends were also up on the wall of prayer. We moved into a new house when I was in senior high school and I remember my dad asking her to not cover the new wall with maps, pictures and prayer requests. So she created a "mobile altar" (you will have to read the book to know more). I thought it was brilliant, and still do!

I cannot emphasize enough the need to read this book. What a privilege to read these pages and gain from a lifetime of focused prayer, study, and deliberate walk with God. It is birthed from a genuine heart that simply wants God's kingdom to be birthed in each of us.

Prayer brings wisdom... Prayer defines us... Prayer transforms us... altering us forever in the altar spaces of God. I am who I am because of a praying family. I believe you will be strengthened, too, as you take the challenge to walk out your personal journey of prayer with God.

I love how my mom phrases it in the preface: "I began to notice the way altars were used, their design and purpose in revealing God to mankind and bringing mankind into relationship with God."

I believe as you read this book, God will reveal defining moments and inspire you. The altar of your heart will be forever changed as you seek God and accept the invitation to

Come and Dine with the King.
Dr. David Rumley, Author—***Transformational Leadership***
Executive Pastor, First Assembly of God
Normal, Illinois

Endorsements

"You hold in your hand a powerful spiritual weapon. It was given by the Spirit of Jesus, to honor His heavenly Father and bring His greater glory into the earth. I have known Elaine Rumley for many, many years. I am blessed to know her as my friend. Not only is she a faithful prophetic voice to the Body of Christ but she is a seasoned woman of God who, in humility, lives the kingdom truths she shares with others. Read this practical guide to learn how to enjoy daily fellowship encounters with the Father. Read it also to be equipped as part of His end time Army which will advance His Kingdom in the earth."

Dr. Walter Fletcher, Contributing Author, *The Revival Study Bible*
Regional Leader
Dallas, Texas

Pastor Elaine Rumley's *Come and Dine with the King* is the most soothing and informative read I have had in quite awhile, and truly a balm for the busy heart…

I love this book, because it took me back to a much slower time, a calmer time in my life. As a teenager, out of respect for the Lord I had established an altar in my room. And every morning, immediately after crawling out of my bed, I would fall to my knees before my altar and pray. It was a small brown cabinet only knee high. I remember my overwhelming excitement when I bought a 10 inch Cross for it, placed it in the center and laid my Bible before it. A little piece of Heaven entered my life that day. And it re-entered my life with Elaine's book…

Though I pray daily, every morning and throughout the day, there is something incredibly personal, intimate and powerful about coming before your own Altar before the Lord. There is such a calming effect. Pastor Elaine has laid out a warm, simple and yet extremely profound plan for one's Altar and personal time with the Lord. Each chapter is like a warm bath of wisdom that soothes away the aches and pains of life's challenges and allows the Holy Spirit to massage in God's Comforts as He wraps us up in His arms… Because of Pastor Elaine and this wonderful book, I am no longer satisfied to rush through life with quick Christian Snacks, but I am returning home to relax and *Come and Dine with the King.*

David M. Humphrey, Author – *Dark Things, The Warrior's Agenda Combat Study Guide, Confessions of a Guardian Angel*
Allen, Texas

"Among the many approaches to prayer and intimacy with God, private altars take a special place in their visibility, personalized location and liturgical association. All of this is no stifling formality in Rev.

Rumley's experience, but a conducive vehicle to enter regularly into a deep and revolutionary encounter with the Lord. It is because of these recurring experiences that altars are offered in *Come and Dine with the King* as an aid to meet with the Lord in a sanctified spot and time – highly recommended reading for personal study and application!"

Dr. Toni Grosshauser
Aumühle, Germany

"Elaine Rumley is a prayer powerhouse and a gifted teacher. Her book, *Come Dine with the King,* is not merely theory on prayer and relationship with God, but gleanings from a lifetime of practicing what she has written about. You will greatly benefit from the practical, life-changing insights this book contains."

Chris & Debbie Lascelles
YWAM Tyler Leadership Team
Creators of *The Ear Bible*

"The book *Come and Dine with the King* written by Elaine Rumley is not only worth reading, but a must read for every Christian who seeks to have a life filled with consistent growth of intimacy with the LORD.

Elaine writes out of the wealth of experience she has consistently gathered and garnished from the table of the LORD every day over the course of many years. She does not give 'a teaching' from studying a passage or a portion or even the entire book of the Bible. She pours out her heart, which is filled with a message from the throne of God.

I am very happy to know that she waited so long, because she continued to nurture this message in her heart and emotions. She has been walking up and down with her LORD in the path of maturity and reality of the Kingdom of God, which she manifests in her personal and public life and ministry.

Her experience of travel and ministry in several countries of the world has added another dimension in this book. And she brings a valuable and treasured delicacy on the table of the LORD as she puts forth the depth of revelation through her ministry experiences.

I have had the personal experience of meeting with her on several occasions in the U.S. and praying with her and ministering with her. Moreover, it was a great honour for me to have her in India with her team and to minister in several places of the Himalayan region. I wholeheartedly endorse this wonderful book by her and I pray that those who read this book will gain another yet higher dimension of walk and depth with the LORD."

Dr. Gautam Silal, Author—*Passion and Purpose, The Prisoner's Cry*
President and Founder,
Asian Mission Outreach, India

In this age of declining prayer life even among the Christian leaders, it is imperative that every believer understands the reason of their very creation and what an altar is. A Creator of lavish love is seeking fellowship with the zenith of His creation human beings. The very place we meet with God is our heart and it is the personal altar of every believer. Rev. Elaine Rumley is uniquely gifted to teach us about the altars. Her intimate relationship with her Creator for over 4 decades brings such a deep revelation, power and prophetic authority. It's time for all of us to bow down our knees in our personal altars and prepare for His coming. The King is coming soon. This book is a must read for the layperson and for clergy as well.

Sam Dewald—**Pastor & President**
World Healing International
Author—*The King is Coming, Pray for the Peace of Jerusalem: A Divine Way for a Blessed Life*

Preface

Four decades have passed since my mother-in-law gave me my first study Bible. Concerned over my need to come to Christ, she had helped pray me into the Kingdom and the baptism of the Holy Spirit. A vibrant teacher of the scriptures, she taught me how to research the Word and exhorted me to set a prayer time to seek the Lord daily, study the Word and be established in a local body of true believers.

I had a deep hunger to know God. As I began to turn the gold edged pages of Genesis, I found myself devouring chapter after chapter of the Word of God. With great simplicity, I prayed for guidance and help to know Him. Almost immediately, I was led to create a place for prayer. My mother-in-law gave me a small table to place in a quiet corner of my dining room. I added my new Bible and a simple candlestick. This was my first early morning "Meeting Place" with God.

I was instructed by the Lord to get up an hour ahead of the family, which meant five o'clock, and spend that time in privacy with Him. I purchased a small daily devotional to focus my thoughts and a spiral note-book to use as my first journal. I had gone from no books to three books and it changed my life forever. The dawning of each day became a great adventure led by the Holy Spirit, as I would greet the Lord, read, pray, listen and write in whatever order He instructed me. I had entered a personal schooling of the Holy Spirit as I daily encountered a great witness of His loving Presence.

In a matter of a few weeks, I had a consistent pattern of prayer at a personal altar and a constant deepening hunger to know the Lord. Out of these one-on-one sessions came inspiration, increased faith and growing personal fellowship with the Holy Spirit. No two mornings were ever the same! My simple altar table had become an oasis of His abiding presence and I knew I knelt on holy ground.

The Lord would convey thoughts to my heart and I would write them in my journal. Sometimes it was only one word, which I would then look up in the dictionary followed by my concordance for increased understanding. I was learning how to be a student, and the Holy Spirit was my faithful Teacher. Later, He taught me to also exhort and encourage others with His Word. In a natural way, I became a scribe for God and a witness of His goodness. My private altar with the Lord began to influence others who were in need of Him.

As I read and searched the Word, I began to notice the way altars were used, their design and purpose in revealing God to mankind and bringing mankind in relationship with God. Altars were set in appropriate order and used by worshipers of every generation. Here was a tangible place of definite encounter and deep revelation.

My study of the scriptures helped me to increase my knowledge and grow in my relationship with God. I was alive in His love and inspired by the Spirit. I understood life was meant to be a great adventure of unveiling His Face and beholding His Glory.

As I daily answered the invitation to *Come and Dine with the King*, I was:

1. Motivated and exhorted to new levels

2. Ushered into God's presence

3. Taught the things of the Spirit

4. Released in the power of the Holy Spirit

5. Educated in the Word of God

6. Enveloped in His Love

7. Strengthened for my daily walk

8. Kept by His grace

9. Anointed to do intercession for others

10. A witness to prayers being answered

Now it is my joy to invite *you* to come and join me at His table. I want to share these concepts with other believers. I bring an earnest request to the Father that each person reading these pages will be strengthened along their journey with God. Please come and join me at the King's Table.

Opening prayer

Father God, I ask that the readers of these anointed pages would come to an ever increasing knowledge of You. May the altars of their hearts be prepared and the eyes of their hearts be opened by the Holy Spirit. Quicken and enlighten Your people, who beseech You like Moses of old, "Lord, let us see Your glory." May they follow on to personally experience the depths of Your love and the resources of Your provision.

In Jesus's Name, Amen.

Prologue

You hold in your hands a brief journey through the Word of God, which can increase your personal walk with Christ for a life time. This book is written to reveal the bountiful table of the Lord which is continuously set before us with a definite invitation from the King of all Kings:

"Come and dine with Me."

The King sets an *exquisite table* with the finest lace, silver and crystal; abundantly filled with the mouth-watering aroma of fresh bread, savory meat, good wine and ripe fruit. This is a *confidential table* where we may share freely with the Godhead in private conversation and intimate words of sweet fellowship. This *life changing table* is available daily to whosoever will, but few there are that find it.

What a fascinating, breathtaking, excruciating journey life can be. I have often commented, "God never said that life would be easy. He did promise it *could* be victorious." In my own experience, such victory is only known through my receiving the sacrifice of His Son at Calvary and my willingness and faithfulness to come to His Table, which has become my *private daily altar* of personal encounter and prayer.

This book is written because the Lord has urged me to share the manner in which He has led me to rise early in the morning with Bible and journal in hand in order to spend my first waking moments always with Him at a small table altar set apart and dedicated as Holy Ground. The Lord promised in Exodus 20:24, "In every place where I record My name and cause it to be remembered, I will come to you and bless you." He has kept His Word! His presence and fellowship has been my initial embrace at every dawn.

I will forever praise God that, for over 40 years, He has brought me to His banqueting table and His banner over me has been love. I prayerfully invite you to *journey and journal* with me through these chapters that we may dine with the King together. Please bring your Bible plus paper and pen, for He will surely speak with you along the way and you will desire to record the words of your King.

Jeremiah 52:33

"Jehoiachin put off his prison garments, and he dined regularly at the king's table all the days of his life."

Table of Contents

Chapter 1 — Begin the Journey

Read Genesis 1-4

Every life has a unique journey! The sharing of that journey can often be a witness to release encouragement, hope and vision to others. Therefore, I delight to take this opportunity as a special time to share some important portions of my walk with God.

I have had the privilege of living and traveling in many nations where I have met with countless members of God's family. We often gathered for fellowship and broke bread together with much thanksgiving and celebration. We welcomed the Lord as our Honored Guest; because He promised that where two or three are gathered in His name, He is present in their midst. Over the decades, I learned that every table of such fellowship became an altar of His grace with the opportunity to share heart to heart, eye to eye and mind to mind the goodness of God.

As I share my testimony, I especially remember the tables of sharing we enjoyed on our first mission trip to Bulgaria in 2001, where our demanding schedule caused us to rigorously travel the countryside. We visited a new city or village every day, as we ministered to ten graduating classes of Bible students across the nation. We usually stayed in homes where no one spoke English, yet in their kind hospitality the love of Christ was exchanged across the coffee table or breakfast table. With many hand gestures and cordial smiles of welcome, our gracious Bulgarian hosts gave us the best of anything they had to make us feel welcome in their homes. Many mission trips later, I am still a witness of the global hospitality of God's family.

I learned that in order to meet the *family* and journey to many foreign places, there was always the necessity of much preparation. Because there was a call to minister, a date to go and a plane to catch, I would set special time aside to accomplish what needed to be done to prepare for the ministry and to care for my family's needs.

It was always a blessing to sit down on the initial airplane flight, fasten my seat belt, take a deep breath and experience the presence of God's peace in my heart; because I knew I was ready to begin the mission and was prepared to serve Him. In the closing moments prior to shutting the door of the aircraft, I often watched to see who might come on board to be seated by me for the journey; after all, there might be a Divine appointment to my right or left. Soon, the stewardess would seal the door and require all passengers to shut off their phones and electronic devices as the plane left the dock. Out on the runway, our international jet would pick up speed as we swiftly taxied to lift off and we were airborne. When I heard the sound of the wheels coming up there was the absolute reality—we had begun the journey.

Now as a part of my journey with the Lord, I have prepared this book and I invite you to come with me and let us share together. We will read and learn about altars from the books of the Bible and observe the divine possibilities of continuous guidance, fellowship and growth in the Holy Spirit because of a personal altar. I will describe the pattern the Lord has given to me to maintain spiritual strength and experience the reality of His presence.

In this sharing, we will use the scriptures as our main reference. Let us start with the book of beginnings which Moses recorded and titled Genesis. From these chapters, I am convinced humanity was formed out of the dust of the ground to know and serve the Living Creator. We understand that when God in centuries past miraculously created the heavens and the earth, there was great preparation, Divine thought and order with exact precision in His plan and purposes.

In the process of creation, the Lord brought forth Adam and placed within Adam's being a piece of the DNA of God. Then He took a portion of Adam's DNA and placed it in His own heart, creating in mankind a longing for identity with his Creator. From the very beginning, God meant for us to live in Him and He would live in us; His heart would be our meeting place and our heart would be His dwelling place. He freely gave to all who would believe a powerful alliance with Himself!!

In Judson Cornwall's book *Things We Adore*[1] he states, "The Genesis account of creation assures us that God spoke everything into existence except persons. In creating Adam, God took of His divine substance and combined it with the dirt of the earth. God then breathed His divine life into this creature enabling man to become a *living soul*." (Genesis 2:7) This makes men and women uniquely different from any other living creature. People are peculiar and superior to all creation. In an unparalleled way, they are the zenith of God's creation and the special enjoyment of God, their Creator. The psalmist understood this, for he wrote, "*For the Lord takes pleasure in His people*." (Psalm 149:4)

It is my desire that we would increase His pleasure as we hear and obey His call to come and dine at the King's Table. In the pages of this book, we will consider every table to be an *altar of meeting*. Therefore, we need to research the question, "What exactly is an altar?"

When we consider an altar, it is a designated and consecrated meeting place with God. It can be a definite area or a table set aside for worship. It does not have to be elaborate or expensive, but it needs to be established through prayer as holy and precious. Our approach to an altar is in the fear of the Lord with a reverence and respect for Who He is.

According to Webster's Dictionary[2] an altar is: 1. A usually raised structure or place on which sacrifices are offered or incense is burned in worship; 2. A table on which the Eucharistic elements are consecrated or which serves as a center of worship or ritual.

As we dig into God's Word, there are seven things I have learned and want us to consider about altars:

1. Each altar in the scriptures has a valuable purpose and reveals a specific personal encounter with a Living God.

2. Altars bring order and substance into our Christian experience.

---

[1] Things We Adore, Judson Cornwell, page 54

[2] Webster's New World Dictionary

3. Altars are a bold witness of our personal faith and they are guarded by the angels of the Lord.

4. Altars are a place of blood sacrifice, a declaration of Christ's death and of our own crucifixion.

5. Altars are a place of mercy and grace with a declaration of God's love for mankind.

6. Altars release warfare and travail for all nations.

7. Altars are a place of worship and holy tangible encounter, with two-way conversation, personal instruction and promised blessings.

Let's enter the scriptures at Genesis and locate the first altar:

Genesis 1:1–"In the beginning God (prepared, formed, fashioned, and) created the heavens and the earth."

The book of Genesis shares the truth about beginnings, birth and the history of mankind's origin. It is written:

The Spirit of the Lord hovered over the chaos of the earth, and God spoke and created all life and substance. He declared each part was good and blessed all of creation to be fruitful and multiply the goodness of what He had made. He placed Adam and the woman in the garden with authority to have dominion, to tend, guard and keep all He had given. And God saw everything that He had made, and behold, it was very good (suitable, pleasant) and He approved it completely. (Genesis 1:31)

God came daily to enjoy His beautiful creation and fellowship with Adam and Eve in true communion as the three of them walked and talked together. This great privilege of open communication lasted for only two brief chapters of the scriptures. In chapter three of Genesis, (Genesis 3:6) we observe the new couple as they gaze at forbidden fruit. The more it took their attention, the greater the pressure of temptation and the enemy encouraged their presumption to be equal to God.

First the woman and then Adam made the choice to disobey God's direct command. Their rebellious actions released a global curse upon the earth and all mankind while their sin stripped them of their position, leaving them naked and undone. God, in His mercy and redemptive power, shed the blood of an animal to make Adam and then Eve long coats of animal skin to cover their nakedness.

The Lord clearly stated the consequences and ramifications of their sin. He forced Adam and Eve from the Garden of Eden and their initial paradise was forever lost; yet God in His mercy gave hope in the promise *"that an Offspring from Eve would come Who would conquer Satan, redeem and fully restore mankind's relationship with God." (Genesis 3:15)*

From that moment of broken relationship with Adam and Eve, a righteous God could only come in fellowship with mankind when they offered a blood sacrifice on an altar of worship to cover their sins. In the Fourth Chapter of Genesis, (Genesis 4:3-5) their fallen, sinful state ushers into position the first mention of an altar. This is Adam's altar and it is apparent he had taught his two grown sons to bring a sacrifice to the family altar. Although the word *altar* is not mentioned, Adam had established times and a location where a blood sacrifice was made to cover their sins. The *first family* would then be able maintain a relationship with Jehovah.

Cain, the eldest son, was a man of the field, for he worked and tilled the ground. We read in Genesis 4:3 that *"Cain brought the fruit of the ground as an offering to the Lord."* However, it is stated that the Lord did not receive Cain's offering. He spoke and warned Cain concerning his angry attitude towards his brother Abel.

In Genesis 4:7, God comes to Cain with a strong statement which he needed to ponder <u>carefully:</u> *"If you do well, will you not be accepted? And if you do not do well, sin crouches at your door; its desire is for you, but you must master it."* Through our study of the scriptures, we have received an expanded understanding that jealousy, envy and anger were present in Cain's heart when he offered his gift to God. In Matthew 5:24 we read the <u>instruction of Jesus to His disciples,</u> *"Leave your gift at the altar and go. First make peace with your brother, and then come back and present your gift."*

There is a real need to guard our hearts and take prompt authority over negative thoughts. II Corinthians 10:5 boldly states that we must bring every thought into captivity and into obedience to Christ. There is tremendous power that can work for us when we let our minds focus in the right direction. There is also the potential of destructive power when we let our minds and imaginations get turned in the wrong direction. A bad attitude held in the heart can escalate into a destructive situation. Cain's bitter thoughts against his brother, along with his refusal to humble himself and hear God's warning, led him to an act of murder!

We need a daily devotional time and a private altar of prayer, because sin in our hearts is a definite fact and not just a slight defect. We must learn to listen to the *checks* of the Holy Spirit to examine our hearts, because if sin rules in us, God's life in us will be diminished or even destroyed. If we choose to let God rule in us by the knowledge of the Word, faithful prayer and worship, then any sin in us will be destroyed. Is it not right and just that *"to whom much is given, much is required"*? (Luke 12:48)

This is neither legalism nor religion. It is a true, marvelous relationship. We need to get a sure grip on the Word of God and agree with truth. Our lives are actually changed by the small rudder of our tongue. Our words and the attitude behind them are either life or death for ourselves and for others; in this regard, we must also include the words we speak in prayer. James 3:2 states it this way, *"For we all often stumble and fall and offend in many things. And if anyone does not offend in speech [never says the wrong things], he is a fully developed character and a perfect man, able to control his whole body and to curb his entire nature."*

In observing Adam's altar, we need to also consider the actions and sacrifice of Abel. Cain's brother Abel was a keeper of sheep and brought the firstborn of his flock and of the fat portions to the altar. The Lord had respect and regard for Abel and for his offering because he was a righteous man. We have a witness in the New Testament, when Jesus warns the scribes and Pharisees to be right with God. He says, *"So that upon your heads may come all the blood of the righteous (those who correspond to the divine standard of right) shed on earth, from the blood of the righteous Abel." (Matthew 23:35)*

Continuing in the New Testament, the scriptures give us a further insight in Hebrews 11:4, *"[Prompted, actuated] by faith Abel brought God a better and more acceptable sacrifice than Cain, because of which it was testified of him that he was righteous [that he was upright and in right standing with God], and God bore witness by accepting and acknowledging his gifts. And though he died, yet [through the incident] he is still speaking."* Abel approached the altar as a man of righteousness with an active faith in God, offering the best lamb of his flock with recognition of his personal need. Therefore, God heard His prayers and received his offering. He was murdered, but centuries later his blood still speaks a clear message to all who read his testimony.

Adam's altar is an ancient marker with an up-to-date reminder concerning our need to approach God in the right manner and with faith. It is also a revelation of God's mercy, patience and goodness as we hear Him warning Cain that he needed to correct himself, because the enemy was at his door. The Lord does not desire that any man should perish and be separated from Him. As a follower of Christ maintaining a daily time with God, we bear witness that it helps us to submit to Truth, receive correction and increased knowledge through His Word.

From the moment the Lord asked me to set up an altar and meet Him at my altar before dawn every morning, I have experienced a living, growing relationship with the Lord. The Holy Spirit has faithfully guided, equipped, comforted, taught, healed and strengthened me. He is the most amazing, empowering Friend; even as Jesus promised He would be in John 16:13-14.

> *But when He, the Spirit of Truth (the Truth-giving Spirit) comes, He will guide you into all the Truth (the whole, full Truth). For He will not speak His own message [on His own authority]; but He will tell whatever He hears [from the Father; He will give the message that has been given to Him], and He will announce and declare to you the things that are to come [that will happen in the future]. He will honor and glorify Me, because He will take of (receive, draw upon) what is Mine and will reveal (declare, disclose, transmit) it to you.*

There are times we sit at His feet and learn of Him, but there is more. We must also take action, for each of us must choose how we are to rise up from that altar and follow Christ. I believe the Lord wants us to live victorious lives, bringing forth good things and steadily becoming stronger to serve Him as we help to lead others. May I suggest it is time to establish the altar of your heart and even an altar in your home.

I am a witness that whether you use a chair, a table or sit on the floor; the Lord will come to your designated place and meet you there in real fellowship. Remember to gather your three books: a Bible, a journal and some book of inspirational devotional material. I would also suggest worship music to begin your sessions with praise and adoration. Keep all of your preparations simple and follow the Spirit's guidance. God values and appreciates a thankful, hungry and spontaneous heart. He is worthy to receive all our gratitude, thanksgiving, adoration and praise. My heart yearns for others to know the precious experience of His presence. I pray that you will begin the journey of a lifetime and never stop!

Please join me in prayer:

Father God, we come to you in the name of your Son Jesus Christ, Who is our perfect sacrifice. We ask for the Holy Spirit to enlighten our understanding and lead us into a new dimension of prayer and fellowship with you. We are hungry to know you, Lord. You have promised that they who hunger and thirst after righteousness shall be fed. (Matthew 5:6) Thank You that we may come to Your abundant table and have the privilege to dine with you. We know you will meet us there daily to share your thoughts and heart with us. In Jesus's name, Amen.

Considerations:

1. We are called to be witnesses of what we believe concerning the Gospel. If we maintain a daily communion with the Lord, we easily share with others the Good News of what the Lord is doing with us. Do we keep our relationship with God current? If we love Him, we will follow Him and be His disciple. Jesus asked the question, *"Why do you call Me, Lord, Lord, and do not [practice] what I tell you?"* (Luke 6:46)

2. In considering the seven things I have personally learned from maintaining a daily altar, I suggest that you have a specific, designated place where you meet with the Lord every day. If you will create such a place of private communication with God and meet with Him daily for 21 days, your life will be forever changed. This takes an initial discipline and change of schedule, but it becomes a wonderful, embracing relationship inspired by the Holy Spirit. People fail to pray because they do not understand how to activate a living relationship with God. The Lord longs for our presence and invites us to come and learn of Him.

    We understand that what we gaze upon is what we become. We need to guard our eyes, ears and heart. What are we focusing on? What are we listening to? Encourage yourself in the Lord by focusing on what is good. In your quiet time, you will learn how to listen to the checks and guidance of the Holy Spirit.

Notes

Notes

Chapter 2 — A Sweet Fragrance

Read Genesis 6-8

In the late 1980's, a few intercessors were gathered with me in a second story base apartment for our weekly prayer session at Ramstein Air Force Base, West Germany. As we began our usual time of sharing and intercession, we sought the Lord for the needs of others and for the nations. Suddenly, I had an amazing experience as I was caught up by the Holy Spirit. In a moment of time, He lifted me high in the heavens and positioned me in outer space. I looked up in wonder at the galaxies and gazed down at the beauty of the huge blue marble called planet Earth.

With amazement, I observed the world from my new location. I realized the atmosphere around me felt thick and everything was strangely quiet. Then suddenly, I heard a thundering voice shouting, "Floodtide! Floodtide! Floodtide on the Earth!" I looked and beheld dark, muddy waves of swiftly flooding waters beginning to dramatically pour across the nations. The dark waves represented false spiritual powers from the East. I watched the filthy waves as they surged westward across the entire earth until there was not even the site of mountain tops! Nothing of the beauty of the nations remained and I could only see the dark, churning waters flooding the world.

In what seemed only a few moments, I saw a lighthouse from the Lord break forth on the east coast of America and stand above the muddy torrents of water. The bright, piercing Light of the lighthouse was beaming into the turbulent sea. At that moment, I was brought instantly from above the earth into the filthy waters. I was totally immersed in the deep waters and from this new position, I could clearly see the one beam of Light, which revealed hundreds of naked human beings threshing against each other, like so many fish caught in a fisherman's net.

Immediately, I was once again taken to a place of observation above the earth, where I witnessed other lighthouses begin to arise in strategic places in the nations. The Word of the Lord came to me saying, "There is coming a day in the earth like Noah's day and only where My Lighthouse stands and My Light pours forth into the great floodtide can there even be the hope of salvation for mankind." The Lord reminded me that He had spoken to me in the early 1970's that I would live to see *the days of Noah*. Therefore, in this chapter, I think it would be good for us to consider *the days of Noah*, as we find our second altar in the book of Genesis.

In the generations following Adam, the world had become very evil and God was weary and grieved at the extreme wickedness of His creation.

Genesis 6:5-7

The Lord saw that the wickedness of man was great in the earth, and that every imagination and intention of all human thinking was only evil continually.

And the Lord regretted that He had made man on the earth and He was grieved at heart.

So the Lord said, I will destroy, blot out, and wipe away mankind, whom I have created from the face of the ground—not only man, [but] the beasts and the creeping things and the birds of the air—for it grieves Me and makes Me regretful that I have made them. (Genesis 6:5-7)

But Noah walked in right relationship with God, because of his faith in a promised Redeemer and the need of a vicarious atonement. In a time of severe worldwide judgment, Noah found grace in God's eyes and was given a set of blueprints with instructions from the Master Architect for every detail of building a massive structure called an ark. This great vessel was 450 feet long, 75 feet wide and 45 feet high. It was to be painted with pitch to waterproof every seam. (It is interesting to me that *pitch* comes from a root word which is translated *atonement*.) [3]

While building and filling the ark with adequate provisions for the family and all the animals, Noah was also preaching righteousness to the all the people of his day.

2 Peter 2:5

And He spared not the ancient world, but preserved Noah, a preacher of righteousness, with seven other persons, when He brought a flood upon the world of ungodly [people].

In the midst of approaching destruction and judgment in the earth, Noah had found favor in the eyes of the Lord and was given a covenant with God that he and his family would live through the raging storms which were to come. He had a promise that when everything they had known was buried under water; God would bring them through safely and usher in a new beginning for the earth for Noah and his descendents. They were not told how long the flood would last, only that they would be secure. It was a walk of faith.

God speaks to us through the written Words of His covenant and we are often amazed at His plans and promises. When we really meditate on His Word, we can be equally amazed at what He didn't say. We find that He keeps us by faith through what has been revealed and we must trust Him by faith for what is yet unknown to us. Our faith and trust must rest in Him alone.

Genesis 7:1

And the Lord said to Noah, Come...

This is the first occurrence of the word *come* in the Bible. I personally believe we are once again living in the days of Noah in a floodtide of darkness. The Lord is still speaking "Come" with the invitation; to separate ourselves, prepare ourselves, be ready to prepare others and come to Him in the privacy of our daily altar for all that we need. Like Noah, we have been chosen in the midst of this generation to receive God's

---

[3] New Unger's Bible Handbook, P.37

blueprints, build places of safety and cities of refuge. Do we recognize this and are we making proper preparations?

In God's timing, Noah, his family and all the animals entered the ark. Then *"the Lord shut them in." (Genesis 7:16)* I can imagine that many of the people may have come to the ark when the rains started and the waters began to rise, but they were too late to get on board. Noah could not open the door to their cries for help and soon there were no more voices outside the ark, only the sound of the rain coming down and surging waves from underground rivers rising up. This was not a local problem, but a worldwide flood; it was a global catastrophe, which lasted a little over a year (371 days).

In time the rains stopped, then the waters began to recede and winds began to blow in a process of drying out the earth. The ark rested on Mount Ararat as the waters went back into their appropriate boundaries and God sent winds to dry out the earth.

Genesis 8:15-22

And God spoke to Noah, saying,

Go forth from the ark, you and your wife and your sons and their wives with you.

Bring forth every living thing that is with you of all flesh—birds and beasts and every creeping thing that creeps on the ground—that they may breed abundantly on the land and be fruitful and multiply upon the earth.

And Noah went forth, and his wife and his sons and their wives with him [after being in the ark one year and ten days]."

"Go forth!" They had waited for the Lord's command! How marvelous that first breath of freedom must have been for Noah, his family and all the animals as they evacuated the ark in an orderly fashion. They broke their year long confinement as they drank in the beauty and breathed the sweet fragrance of a freshly washed Earth. There are many seasons to life and we can often feel limited and isolated. In our hearts we too long for freedom. However, we can rest assured and trust the Lord that in His perfect timing He will also say to us "Go forth!"

Every beast, every creeping thing, every bird—and whatever moves on the land—went forth by families out of the ark. (Genesis 8:19)

Noah came out of the ark with his family, alongside every creature on the ark with their offspring. What a moment of new beginning, hope and pageantry that must have been as they emptied that great, three-story ship. It was a beautiful picture of unity and support to begin a brave new world. I would love to have a video replay! I thank Creator God for new beginnings and the strength of others who join with us!

Continuing in Genesis 8:20-22

[20]And Noah built an altar to the Lord and took of every clean [four-footed] animal and of every clean fowl or bird and offered burnt offerings on the altar.

²¹ When the Lord smelled the pleasing odor [a scent of satisfaction to His heart], the Lord said to Himself, I will never again curse the ground because of man, for the imagination (the strong desire) of man's heart is evil and wicked from his youth; neither will I ever again smite and destroy every living thing, as I have done.

²²While the earth remains, seedtime and harvest, cold and heat, summer and winter, and day and night shall not cease.

Notice that the very first thing Noah accomplished was to build an altar and have a blood sacrifice on that altar with every clean animal and bird. He and his family humbly worshipped God. The sounds and activities of sin had been destroyed, the earth was strangely quiet and the smells of pure worship were rising to Heaven. God was receiving ministry that satisfied His heart. Proverbs 15:29 says, *"The Lord is far from the wicked, but He hears the prayer of the [consistently] righteous (the upright, in right standing with Him.)"*

You and I have the daily opportunity to freely come to our altars of devotion, where with thanksgiving we can lift a sweet fragrance of worship to the Lord. The amazing truth is when we truly worship Him, He pours blessings back upon us in forms of guidance, healing and answered prayer. Through these spiritual transactions, God becomes more tangible; we continuously grow and want to know Him more deeply.

We are told that Noah was a man who walked with God, which implies a daily commitment to be with Him. To walk with God is a chosen way of life and precious fellowship for an intercessor. It does not just happen; it is a deliberate daily choice with a pattern of love, respect, faith and service which we establish as believers.

If we do indeed live in *the days of Noah*, how do you and I establish an altar with a sweet fragrance to God? It is not about a certain religious formula of three steps, but a pattern of true relationship continuously led by the Holy Spirit. The Spirit will help us to set boundaries, to fast, make progress in prayer and keep *on target* in our private times with the Lord. This in turn releases more faith, order and substance into our daily Christian experience.

Andrew Murray in his book titled Andrew Murray on Prayer writes, "In an elder's prayer meeting, a brother asked the question: 'What is the cause of so much prayerlessness? Is it not unbelief?' The answer was: 'Certainly; but then comes the question—what is the cause of that unbelief?'

When the disciples asked the Lord Jesus: *'Why could not we cast [the devil] out?'* His answer was, *'Because of your unbelief.'* He went further and said: *'Howbeit this kind goeth not out but by prayer and fasting.'* (Matthew 17:19-21) If our life is not one of self-denial, of fasting, of letting go of the world, choosing discipline and anointed prayer which lays hold of Heaven, then true faith is difficult to exercise. Instead, we may live a life according to our flesh and not according to the Spirit. It is in this that we find the basis of prayerlessness, of which we complain. Andrew Murray continued, 'As we came out of the meeting, a brother said to me: 'That is the whole difficulty; we wish to pray in the Spirit and at the same time walk after the flesh, and this is impossible.'"[4]

---

[4] Andrew Murray, Andrew Murray on Prayer, P. 156

For myself, I know as a new Christian my greatest need was to be baptized in the Holy Spirit. However, at that time as a new convert, I did not understand my need. How grateful I am that other intercessors who had walked closely with the Lord for many years knew my need and prayed for me to receive this vital experience. This fact alone has caused me to pray for many others to receive the baptism of the Holy Spirit. For it is the Holy Spirit Who has taught, led, comforted, convicted, protected and strengthened me in every way. When I received the baptism, I did not even know Christian terminology; but others prayed for me. God answered those prayers with power from on high and I was given a prayer language in the Holy Spirit. He poured a new strength into my life and I was forever ruined for anything less than the power and presence of the Living God.

Jesus promised in John 14:26:

> *But the Comforter (Counselor, Helper, Intercessor, Advocate, Strengthener, Standby),the Holy Spirit, Whom the Father will send in My name [in My place, to represent Me and act on My behalf], He will teach you all things. And He will cause you to recall (will remind you of, bring to your remembrance) everything I have told you.*

The baptism of the Holy Spirit made me hungry to know God. I began to devour the Word of God from cover to cover, from Genesis to Revelation. I was looking for the Lord and searching diligently to know Him. In those early days, He encouraged me to raise up my first altar and meet Him there every morning before dawn. I had a growing young family which required my full attention and before the sun or the family would rise, I would quietly get out of bed and go to my altar to worship the Lord with total concentration. I cannot put into words the benefits of those early morning hours!

Over the years my altar has developed into a larger sphere of intercession and covers

many lives, ministries and nations. I have been led to create photo albums filled with prayer needs, pictures and ministry brochures. I have also gained a fifth book, my World Atlas, so that I can lay hands on the nations. This helps wonderfully when we are interceding for missions or a ministry in another location. Although my sphere of spiritual influence has increased, the basic foundation of my altar has never changed.

I come daily to the *Table of the Lord* and minister to Him as my first love. I listen and receive the instruction of the Holy Spirit because each day can flow a little differently. I take a few minutes to listen to music, get settled in my own spirit and minister to Him with praise. I will take my journal and write down the very first thoughts the Spirit gives to me. Sometimes He sends me to a *word search* in my Bible concordance, some mornings He speaks directly and I write down all He shares with me, and then there are mornings He will show me a special scene and I draw out what He is sharing. For instance, He often shows me a fruitful tree or a palm tree and begins to share with my heart what that tree represents. These are visual object lessons which I can remember through the day and ponder in my heart.

I invite you to come join me at His marvelous table. I pray for the Spirit to lead you forward in your special walk with Jesus Christ.

Father God,

We come with thanksgiving, respect and love to your altar. I believe there are new concepts and insights which you are writing on the hearts of those who read these pages. I ask You to help each reader to draw closer to You, even as You have often used others and their writings to help me come nearer to You. Rescue them from the chaos and noise of this generation. May they change the conditions and atmosphere around them and break through with a sweet aroma to please and bless You. I ask You that each one of them would develop and grow in a dynamic daily walk of fellowship with You. May we be lighthouse builders, sending the Light forth to a desperate generation.

In Jesus's Name, Amen

Considerations:

1. I think it is time for us *to come* — enter into a closer walk with the Lord, build our altar and establish what He wants done. Then we will be prepared to *go forth* to honor Him and share His goodness. Our personal altar and close fellowship with the Lord will give hope to others. We are the Light of this world, I pray we will shine brightly for Him in this hour.

2. Perhaps you or someone you care about is in turbulent waters, like the muddy floodtide. As we spend time with the Lord, His Word and Presence become a safe gift of peace to our souls. He empowers us to be a witness to others. Let us pray fervently for the salvation of souls and that they may enter His peace and the joy of His Salvation.

3. Noah believed God's instructions and made preparations. The Lord brought the animals and then told Noah when there was only one more week to be ready. What preparations do we need to make? If we draw nigh to God now, the promise is He will draw nigh to us and instruct us. I encourage you to raise up your altar of prayer and worship. If judgment comes, God's mercy will be extended to those who love Him.

Notes

Chapter 3 — The Lord, My Provider

Genesis 11-22

When I began to come to the King's Table as a brand new believer, I was hungry to learn about the things of God and excited to have daily fellowship with the Lord Himself. Certainly, it was a new discipline to get up every morning before dawn, but God gave me the grace to obey His call to *arise and come*. He would awaken me and I would immediately arise. After I got up, washed my face and sat down on the floor by my small altar in our dining room, the Holy Spirit would begin to guide me through our special time together. He proved Himself again and again to be my faithful Teacher. He certainly had my full attention, since no two mornings were ever the exactly the same. The leadership of the Holy Spirit Himself was the Source of my continuous excitement in a growing friendship with God.

I began to sense the personality of the Holy Spirit as our association grew; some mornings were very quiet, as I felt a stillness to read, focus and meditate on the Word. Often I would journal my thoughts and pray them out loud to the Lord.

In a few months, I had devoured every chapter of my new *Scofield Reference Bible* from cover to cover. There were mornings full of private instruction, as the Spirit would give me the focused thought of one single word. He taught me how to follow that word through my dictionary and cross reference it through my concordance. Within a year, I was also introduced to *Strong's, Vine's, Matthew Henry's Commentary* and other study materials, as the Holy Spirit taught me to be a faithful student of the Word.

In my studies, I found out that God loves details, order and simplicity. He is a God of timing, seasons, purposes and plans. He is Father, Mother and perfect Friend! The more I learned, the more deeply I hungered to know more. My hour of morning retreat with Him seemed like only a moment and I began to find ways to incorporate more time to sit at His feet, yet fully accomplish my busy schedule as a wife and mother. I was so hungry to know and learn more about Him that during the day, whenever I could find time, I would sit down and pick up the Word! I kept an old hymnal by my kitchen sink and sang to the Lord in English and in the Spirit as I worked! Truly, He lightened and brightened my day.

These were the early days when the Holy Spirit began to train me to hear His voice and move in the prophetic. He would give me a note of encouragement to share with someone or He would speak to my heart about calling someone in the church to encourage them in their walk of faith. Every single time, those *rhema* words were received with joy and thanksgiving. These thankful responses, in turn, caused my faith and trust to grow.

Today, we have amazing information stored on websites with expansive studies at our fingertips. However, even with the great advancements of technology, one thing has not changed: It takes quiet, reverent friendship —, not just information — to truly know and experience the Living God. Everything about Him in us must be a faith-built heart connection. There is an old saying that "to know Him is to love Him and if we love Him, we will serve Him." Selah! (Pause and think about that.)

Andrew Murray writes in *Andrew Murray on Prayer:*

> The place and power of prayer in the Christian life is too little understood. As long as we view prayer simply as the means of maintaining our own Christian lives, we will not fully understand what it is really suppose to be. But when we learn to regard it as the highest part of the work entrusted to us—the root and strength of all other work—we will see that there is nothing we need to study and practice more than the art of prayer.5

In the Book of Genesis, there was a man named Abraham who was called the friend of God. He was an altar builder, a man of faith, obedient to the Lord's command, a visionary who miraculously became the Father of many nations. He lived his life of faith and friendship to fulfillment, as he learned by personal experience to wait on the Lord's timing and obey the Lord's instructions. Abraham dared to believe that with God all things were possible.

Abraham was first known as Abram, meaning *an exalted father.*6 His father, Terah, chose several members of the family living in Ur of the Chaldeans and they started out for the land of Canaan. However, he stopped their travels part way in the area of Haran and years later he died there. At his death, the Lord spoke to Abraham and told him it was in his best interest and a definite advantage to leave the area and proceed on to Canaan. Abraham packed up his belongings and faithfully moved everything and everyone to the new territory. What would be there? He did not know. Who would be there? God!

In Genesis 12:1-3 (NKJV) the Lord had spoken eight "wills" to Abram:

(Emphasis mine)

> *Leave your country and your people. Leave your father's family. Go to the land I will show you.*
>
> *I will make you into a great nation.*
>
> *I will bless you.*
>
> *I will make your name great.*
>
> *You will be a blessing to others.*
>
> *I will bless those who bless you.*
>
> *I will put a curse on anyone who calls down a curse on you.*

---

5 Andrew Murray, Andrew Murray on Prayer, P. 315

6 Dakes Annotated Reference Bible, KJV, P. 22

All nations on earth <u>will</u> be blessed because of you.

As Abraham traveled, he did not choose a direct route, but instead chose to follow the flow of the rivers to get to Canaan. This was a wise choice, because as they continued on the journey his stock and servants stayed strong with a good water supply. They traveled to Shechem and stopped by a huge terebinth tree. In those days, altars were built of rough stones or earth. They were often raised up in a grove of trees or established by a large tree. The altar stood as a symbol of communion with Jehovah, a place of blood sacrifice, and it often commemorated a personal encounter with the Lord.

As we consider these altars and what they represented to Abraham, may we also be aware that every believer will have their own altars of personal encounter. Therefore, as we study these passages in Genesis, let us consider well the ways that the Lord searched Abraham's heart and watched his reactions.

For example, there was an encounter in *Genesis 12:7:*

> *Then the Lord appeared to Abram and said, I will give this land to your posterity. So Abram built an altar there to the Lord, Who had appeared to him.*

In *Genesis 12:8* Abram moved to Bethel (the house of God) and he chose to establish another altar where he called on the Lord.

I believe that as it was true for Abram, so it is true for us; there is the need to set the vision and purpose of an altar tangibly before us, honoring God for Who He is in our lives and reminding us daily of our need to honor Him and connect with His purposes. An altar invites His Presence, causes us to pause in our busy schedules and take time to worship and praise the Lord while we remember the high cost of our salvation.

In our busy generation, the daily demands and pressures of life have driven out the fellowship of the Holy Spirit. We have scheduled God into our calendars in the *mini-bites* of a five minute devotional or a few verses of scripture with a quick, *Praise the Lord! Done my duty for the day, now here I go into the real world!*

There is also the fact that we often feel as pressured by attending meetings at the local church as we do by our job or workplace. These things ought not to be. Is it possible, that instead of knowing God, we have filled ourselves with teaching and information about God? We try to find our way through the maze of accountabilities until there is a "serious suddenly" in our lives and we realize we are void of power and totally worn out. We cry out for Him and question where God is and whether there is any hope that He can change our current difficulty. Then we find ourselves searching for someone — yes, anyone — who is in touch with God.

The pace of our generation and our demanding situations are just two of the reasons why I so fervently believe in a tangible space, a genuine location in our home, where we connect in true relationship! Our daily faithfulness to Him will literally birth a place of Holy Ground, where God's Presence is embraced and He abides with us and our family.

Life changes and, when the shakings come, we need this place of stability to work from and with confidence we can experience the comfort of our best Friend, the Holy Spirit. This is also tremendously important in ministering to others in need. Hundreds of times, I have carried my cell phone to my altar location and prayed for others who were in crisis. From that faith-filled position, the Lord has worked wonders, released miracles of deliverance, and answered prayer even when the person on the other end of the line was halfway around the world.

Apparently, Abram felt the same way about his altar, and the scriptures call him the *friend of God*. (James 2:23) What were the dynamics that produced such a deep personal relationship? In studying his life, we see that he continually chose companionship with the Father as he maintained his daily walk, cried out in prayer and communed with the Lord. In the pattern of his travels, it is recorded that wherever he pitched his tent, there he chose to build an altar to the Lord. In that hallowed place, he called upon the King of the Universe, who was his best Friend. Certainly there were ordinary days, but there were also spectacular encounters — divine appointments that deeply stirred his faith and activated this friendship to new levels.

I am reminded that years ago, as a brand new believer, I was walking in simple obedience to His invitation to meet Him every morning. He helped me to rise up early and come to my altar to greet the dawning of each new day. I wanted to know the Creator of that dawn more than anything else. My hunger and passion to *know* became my alarm clock and urged me to *arise*!

One morning as I sat quietly before Him, I saw His arms come through the wall in front of me and appear right above my altar. As I gazed in amazement at the scars wrapped in glorious Light, Jesus began to speak to my heart. He asked me many searching questions and then waited for my answers. Would I be faithful? Would I trust and follow Him? Was I willing to lay down my life for the Gospel? These were serious questions and He waited patiently for my answers. I did not realize the terminology of *covenant* at that moment of time; I only knew that the One Who had given me life, love, joy and hope wanted me to be faithful and firmly committed to Him. After all these years, I can still see His arms outstretched to me and hear His questions reverberating in my soul. Altars are places of personal encounter, developing friendship and deep commitment.

Many hundreds of years ago, Abraham understood his need of such an altar and the Lord met with him again and again. In Genesis 15:5, *"the Lord spoke to Abram voicing the assurance He was his shield and great reward and his descendents would be like the stars in the sky."*

In *Genesis 17:2-14*, Abram is given a new covenant, his name is changed to Abraham, the Father of many nations and he is instructed to circumcise all the males in his camp as a sign of his covenant with God. The Lord also blesses Sarai and gives her a new name. Now she will be called *Sarah*, which means *princess*. The Lord, Who holds the seasons in His hand, sets a specific boundary of time and says the child of covenant blessing shall come within the year. When the visitation with the Lord was over, Abraham immediately acts upon it and obeys the instructions. A blood covenant is established throughout his entire household.

In Genesis 18:1-8, as Abraham rests in the door of his tent, an ordinary day becomes a brilliant encounter with the Lord. He greets the arrival of guests from heaven; two angels and the Angel of the Lord drop by for lunch. Abraham washes their feet, serves them a good meal and shares fellowship. Once again, the pledge is given that the child shall come.

The visitors prepare to leave and go on to their mission, but Abraham is not ready to say good-bye and walks on in deep conversation with the Lord. The Lord decides that because Abraham is the friend of God, He will share with him what He is about to do in the valley of Sodom and Gomorrah. Hearing the purpose of His coming, Abraham reasons with the Lord and petitions him to not destroy the righteous with the wicked. In this passage we have our first recorded intercession for a city and region. With great respect, Abraham approaches the Lord and stands in the gap for a sinful people.

Genesis 18:32

> *And he said, Oh, let not the Lord be angry, and I will speak again only this once. Suppose ten [righteous people] shall be found there. And [the Lord] said, I will not destroy it for ten's sake."*

Abraham's daily altar had given him the authoritative intercessory position to pray to God on behalf of others, even to the needs of an entire region. We understand — by the judgment that came to the cities — that ten righteous could not be found, but the intimate boldness of Abraham's travail demonstrates to us the results and confidence birthed out of a daily altar relationship.

Your personal altar will build up your faith and personal walk with God. You will identify with His heart on behalf of others who are in need. Serving the Lord in prayer by the anointing of the Spirit pays rich dividends; it releases boldness, righteousness, revelation and opportunities to deliver souls and territorial regions from the grasp of the enemy. Our purpose is always to love as He loves and build what He is building which is *The Kingdom*.

There is a powerful declaration concerning intercessory prayer which we need to consider in Job 22:30: "He will even deliver the one [for whom you intercede] who is not innocent; yes, he will be delivered through the cleanness of your hands". Wow! What a position of authority is granted to those who seek the Lord on behalf of others.

We find another bold declaration filled with promise in Psalm 24:3-5

> *Who shall go up into the mountain of the Lord? Or who shall stand in His Holy Place?*

> *He who has clean hands and a pure heart, who has not lifted himself up to falsehood or to what is false, nor sworn deceitfully,*

> *He shall receive blessing from the Lord and righteousness from the God of his salvation.*

It is recorded in Genesis 21:2-6 "that Isaac the child of promise has been born and the joy of fulfillment has come." After about three years, Hagar and her son are removed from the camp. Sarah comes to Abraham and requires the separation when she sees Ishmael mocking Isaac. Her request deeply grieves Abraham until the Lord instructs him to agree with his wife. God reminds Abraham that his descendants would be called only through the son of covenant blessing, Isaac. (Genesis 4:28-31)

Abraham immediately obeys God, which is a bold witness to our own hearts. (Romans 9:7) Only because of his solid relationship and his walk of obedience could Abraham, yield to the counsel of the Lord when it was so personally painful. May we be encouraged to trust and obey even when it is hard!

This passage has encouraged me many times:

Psalm 62:5-8

> *My soul, wait only upon God and silently submit to Him; for my hope and expectation are from Him.*
>
> *He only is my Rock and my Salvation; He is my Defense and my Fortress, I shall not be moved.*
>
> *With God rests my salvation and my glory; He is my Rock of unyielding strength and impenetrable hardness and my refuge is in God!*
>
> *Trust in, lean on, rely on, and have confidence in Him at all times, you people; pour out your hearts before Him. God is a refuge for us (a fortress and a high tower). Selah [pause, and calmly think of that]! " (Psalm 62:5-8)*

Continuing the journey in Genesis Chapter 21: 32-33, Abraham settled a dispute with his neighbor Abimelech over a well and planted a tamarisk tree at Beersheba where he called on the name of the Everlasting God. As I have mentioned, it was typical in his day that a grove of trees could also be a place of altar. In this case, Abraham made a public statement of his faith and others were able to join with him in worshiping God. Once we have established our own altar, it follows that we will want prayer times when others can enter and join with us.

Matthew Henry makes this comment:

> *"Abraham, being now in a good neighborhood, stayed a great while there. There he made not only a constant practice, but an open profession of his religion. There he called on the name of the Lord, as the everlasting God; probably in the grove he planted, which was his place of prayer. Abraham kept up public worship, in which his neighbors might join. Good men should do all they can to make others so. Wherever we sojourn, we must neither neglect nor be ashamed of the worship of Jehovah.*[7]

As we move into Chapter 22, Abraham encounters the biggest test of his faith and friendship with God.

Genesis 22:1-2

> *"After these events, God tested and proved Abraham and said to him,*
>
> *Abraham! And he said, Here I am*
>
> *[God] said, Take now your son, your only son Isaac, whom you love, and go to the region of Moriah; and offer him there as a burnt offering upon one of the mountains of which I will tell you.*

Abraham set his face toward Moriah believing that God would provide. (Genesis 22:8) and without hesitation he obeyed the Lord's command. He prepared all that would be needed, gathered some servants

---

[7] Matthew Henry Commentary, Vol.I,P.59

and took the three day journey. When they came close to the mountain, he told <u>his servants to camp as he made this simple statement of faith,</u> *"I and the young man will go yonder and worship and come again to you."(Genesis 22:5)*

Abraham took the wood, fire, knife and rope as he declared by faith to Isaac that God would provide the lamb. They climbed and arrived at the exact place the Lord had told Abraham. There they built an altar and set the wood in order for the fire. As Isaac yielded in trust to his father, he allowed himself to be tied and placed on the altar as the sacrifice.

When Abraham lifted the knife to slay his son, "the Angel of the Lord stopped him and said, 'Abraham, You were willing to give Me your only son without begrudging it, now I know you fear and revere God.'" When Abraham looked up, there was a ram nearby, trapped in a thicket and this animal supplied by God became their sacrificial offering to the Lord. Abraham named this altar of personal sacrifice *The Lord Will Provide*.

We may seldom think of how our faith in God has the power to release a sweetness of friendship to His heart. Can we truly grasp that He, too, has needs and desires? Did He not make us for Himself? Man was created to have friendship with his Creator.

Let us consider three questions.

1) Can we, out of loving obedience in our relationship with Him, actually encourage God Himself?

2) How did God feel when a man of the dust was willing, without any debate, to trust and agree with Him to this level of sacrificial action?

3) In our own hearts, are we aware of any lack of obedience or trust?

The Lord promises that the power of Abraham's faith will reach through the centuries and release a blessing upon a multitude of descendents. Through Abraham's Seed, Jesus Christ, all the nations shall be blessed. Because of this altar builder's faith and the strength of God's Provision, we too are blessed and can possess the gates of our enemies! Somebody ought to shout, "Yes, Lord!"

Question: Are you building your altar yet? Can your personal altar leave a legacy of answered prayer and faith to your family, friends, church, community and beyond?

Over the years of my journey with God, I have moved from place to place and it has required the establishing of many altars. My first was the small table in my dining room in North Carolina, for a season in Kansas I used a recliner in my living room, in

Alabama it was a private closet in the master bedroom, and in Germany, my living room coffee table became Holy Ground. Later, we moved to larger living quarters with a fourth bedroom and I was given the privilege of my first private prayer room which was named "My Glory Room," and this altar released a special training season in my walk with God.

I was working with a Christian women's organization as their Bible study and prayer leader across Western Europe. There were many leadership prayer needs and constant individual requests across the network of membership. In my new *Glory Room*, the Lord guided me to establish prayer walls. I placed lists of needs, maps and locations, photographs and scriptures on the four walls of my prayer room. I brought in worship music, a comfortable piece of carpet, my Bible and a journal. Here in this private chamber, I would seek the Lord and worship Him until I had a sense of His guidance. I would rise up and go from map to scripture to prayer lists as the Spirit led me. I would lay hands on these needs and release my faith to the Lord for His answers. In a matter of weeks, I was receiving many praise reports that the situations had been answered and needs had been tangibly met by the Lord. I realized there was a definite power release when I set the vision before me and prayed in agreement with the Holy Spirit. He was teaching me His victorious ways.

The Holy Spirit continued to guide and provide understanding of where to pray, when to pray and how to pray. He kept me in balance with the Word, worship, church ministry and home Bible studies; but always my early morning altar was a tangible place of His grace. The Lord has assured me that my altars will stand and continue to speak down through the years! I could not ask for more!

Now I am excited to invite you to come, taste and see that the Lord is good. May I suggest to you that life and busy schedules will never slow down! Out of love for Him, we must make the time to seek His face and when we do, He will amaze us with the grace of His friendship and the anointing He releases to handle the rest of our schedule!

Please pray with me:

Father God, I hear your invitation resonating with faith in my heart. At your request Lord, I come with my needs, desires and yes, even my failures. Forgive me for every way I have denied you access to my heart and life. I choose to follow You into a new season of personal relationship and friendship. I thank You that You are the God of new beginnings! Fully establish Your Word in me. I choose to open my heart even as I ask You to bring a fresh work of the Holy Spirit into my life. I want to know You and enter into a stronger relationship with You. Show me how I can choose daily altar time with you and truly fellowship in Your love. Please lead me in new patterns of victorious living. Lord, I come believing You will teach me how I can raise up my altar of worship and prayer.

In Jesus's name, Amen.

Considerations:

1. The more we fellowship with the Lord, the better we will know and understand ourselves. The Holy Spirit is a Revealer of hearts. The Lord does not condemn us, but He does correct us in order that we may experience increase and blessings. It takes courage to change, but there are great benefits in obedience.

2. Abraham was a man of faith, an altar builder, an intercessor and called the friend of God. We are called to walk as his seed in the Earth. These characteristics of Abraham need to be developed in our lives through earnest prayer, worship and study. Our faithful diligence will establish increase in the Kingdom and make us ready to walk in our full destiny. Aren't you wanting more in your relationship with God. Activate your faith by pursuing Him in earnest prayer. I know He is waiting to hear your voice!

3. If prayer is our "highest work," how do we begin to learn to pray?
Get into a private place where you can honestly respond to the Lord. Ask the Lord for His heart of love and compassion to be your portion. The Holy Spirit has been given to teach us the ways of God. He inspires and equips us to pray. We go beyond intellect and personal feelings to flow and pray with confidence in the Spirit. Read again I Corinthians 12-14 and realize the power of God, Who dwells within you, to get the work done! Then spend time with Him in true fellowship and pray much in the Spirit. Jude 20 gives us understanding, "But you, beloved, build yourselves up [founded] on your most holy faith [make progress, rise like an edifice higher and higher], praying in the Holy Spirit."

Notes

Chapter 4— Wells, Pillars, Pits and Palaces

Genesis 25:7-8

*The days of Abraham's life were 175 years. Then Abraham's spirit
was released and he died at a good (ample, full) old age,
an old man satisfied and satiated and he was gathered to his people.*

We have witnessed in the chapters of Genesis that the patriarch Abraham was indeed the friend of God as he traveled and pitched his tent in different locations. In each place of his pilgrimage, he consistently took the initiative to establish a personal altar. There appears to have been a true longing within his being for divine fellowship and guidance. Since meeting with God was a priority, Abraham did not wait for the Lord to instruct or command him to establish an altar. Instead, he determined to raise up a place of worship where he could freely speak to God.

Dick Eastman wrote in his book *No Easy Road,* "The more we stand in a friend's presence, the more we understand his personality. In growing to know this friend, we grow to know his will. Thus it is with children of God. Often we bring petitions to God, voicing them with boldness at His throne. Seldom do we talk of simply waiting in His presence."[8]

This longing for God's face is painted with bold strokes on my own heart. After all, isn't that what friends do? Don't friends set a table, fill it with great food and look forward to sharing time together? In our day it is true that a quick text message, a voice mail, a phone call or an e-mail allow certain levels of communication. But gathering around a table with face to face conversation is much more satisfying to the soul, because breaking bread together allows the development of true relationship.

The vivid brush strokes of longing for God's presence came into my own heart after I was filled with the Holy Spirit. I realized that I had come into a relationship of the highest kind and the Spirit drew me to spend time alone with God. When the sun was rising, while family still slept, I sat quietly by my new altar, reading a devotional or continuing through the scriptures. At the prompting of the Holy Spirit, I would begin to write down my thoughts and feelings. The devotional, the scriptures and the journaling helped me to know my own heart, made God alive and began to give me a personal revelation of His absolute love for me. The scriptures became more alive as spiritual things became very real and vibrant in my life. There were mornings when I tangibly knew I had *kissed the face of God.*

The patterns of my daily life changed as I spent my first waking moments in His presence. Certainly there were many days of simple faithfulness as I studied and learned more about Him. Then there were life

---

8 Dick Eastman, No Easy Road, P.97

changing experiences initiated by the Lord, when He brought forth tangible encounters with His presence and revealed His will for my life. I do want to mention that I never asked the Lord for the great revelations and insights. However, I have told Him I am available for whatever He chooses to share and for the disclosure of whatever I need to be victorious in my life or on behalf of others. The Lord has always come for Divine purposes and He still does.

My prayer altar had brought me to a place of deep recognition of the Lord. Encountering His glory truly transformed me and released a new level of communication in the Spirit. As I met with the Lord, I recognized that knowing, growing and learning about Him became the measure of a fulfilled, happy, vibrant life. I was often challenged by the written Word and the *rhema* word to identify with His heart and thoughts. I agree with the testimony of many others down through time that truly never has a man lived or spoken like this Man!

In this chapter, I want to observe to what degree Abraham's lifestyle of altar building, prayer, fellowship, and faithful worship became a spiritual heritage to his descendents after he was gone. Let us take this section to consider the altars of Abraham's seed: Isaac, Jacob and Joseph.

Isaac's altar—

We find Abraham's son Isaac meditated on the things of God. Through the years of his family sojourning, he had grown up with the privilege of altar worship and the close observation of his father's steadfast faith. We find that Isaac sought the Lord diligently in prayer for his wife to come into his life. The Lord answered his cry when his father Abraham's servant, Eliezer, miraculously returned from the land of Mesopotamia with the beautiful Rebekah. Isaac loved Rebekah and she comforted him, but as years went past, they found themselves without children. For an extended season, Isaac sought God's intervention and the Lord answered by giving Rebekah twin boys, whom they named Esau and Jacob.

Abraham passed away at a full old age and left all his wealth to Isaac. A famine came to the land and God spoke to Isaac instructing him where he was to stay temporarily. He declared His favor and blessing rested upon Isaac and his seed because of Abraham's obedience to His commands. Isaac obeyed the Lord's instructions and despite the famine he became a great man with much wealth, including flocks, herds and servants. He dwelt with contentment in the land, tangibly witnessing the favor of God upon his life.

Isaac was focused on a special project as he went about the land restoring the old wells which Abraham's servants had dug. The scriptures state that the Philistines had closed these wells and filled them with earth, making them nonfunctional. Isaac re-established the blessing of a water supply and decreed each well would be called by the original name his father had given to it. In taking back what the enemy had stolen, Isaac proved his respect for his earthly father Abraham and blessed those people who were yet to come with a good water supply.

Isaac encountered God and received a unique blessing from Him at the well of Beersheba. Afterwards he pitched his tent, dug a well and built an altar there, where he called on the name of the Lord. As the seed of Abraham, Isaac had definite encounters, received God's promises and walked in covenant blessings. How did Isaac's testimony affect the next generation of Abraham's seed?

Jacob's pillars and altars—

When Isaac was old, at Rebekah's explicit instruction, Jacob craftily stole the blessings of his brother Esau. This action created great hatred in Esau's heart and he began to speak of killing Jacob as soon as their father passed away. This would be the only way the original inheritance could be returned to him. Rebekah overheard these threatening words and determined Jacob must leave until the anger of his brother was diminished. She decided on a plan and discussed this with Isaac. Jacob was called to meet with his father, who instructed him to travel 400 miles to his uncle's house in Padan-aram to find his wife. (Genesis 27)

Jacob went out immediately on his journey and when the sun began to set, he made a bed in the wilderness with a stone as his pillow. He began to dream of a great ladder between Heaven and Earth with angels going and coming. The Lord stood beside him and made a covenant with him, declaring that Jacob's children would inherit that very piece of land. There was a promise that through his children, all the nations of the Earth would be blessed. Jacob established a pillar of memorial at that exact location, declaring the place to be sacred. This pillar truly became an altar for him, because he had experienced God's presence. He pledged to come back to this holy place if the Lord would keep him and allow him to return in peace to his father's house. (Genesis 28:11-22)

Following this dramatic, personal encounter, the Word says Jacob went cheerfully and briskly on his way to Haran. He did not know it would take nearly 20 years before he returned at the Lord's instruction with his large family, along with accumulated flocks and herds. (Genesis 29-31)

On his journey home, the Lord wrestled with Jacob and changed his name to Israel, for he had contended with God. Jacob called this location Peniel, which means *I have seen God face to face*. He was now spiritually prepared to return home, but he was concerned about his brother Esau's wrath. Jacob established a strategy of gifts sent before him, his family, servants, herds and flocks to prepare and ease the way for his homecoming. The Lord answered his prayers for when the brothers met, they embraced each other and relationship was restored.(Genesis 32:24-31)

After these experiences, Jacob came to such a dimension of peace and blessing that he chose to raise up an altar and called it *El-Elohe-Israel*. This name meant, *God-the God of Israel*. The Lord was no longer just the God of Abraham and Isaac, but Jacob took ownership of his faith and declared He was the God of Israel. (Genesis 33:20)

Later, Jacob was instructed to come full circle and return to the pillar he had raised up when he left home many years before. He was to take a new step of faith, build an altar there and call it El Bethel, where God revealed Himself. (Genesis 35:7) In Jacob's day, wherever there were places of spiritual encounter, the location would be marked by a stone pillar or a memorial would be erected, anointing oil was poured out and the place became a marked location of worship because of God's visitation. We could call each of these locations places or altars of remembrance and encounter. In the Word of God, we find this promise, "...In every place where I record My name and cause it to be remembered I will come to you and bless you."(Exodus 20:24) This is an important insight for us to consider, for we are promised that when we establish a definite location where we meet with the Lord on a regular basis, He will record His name, come to us and bless us there. What a wonderful declaration of His personal visitation and continuous presence, because He longs to meet with us.

Many years ago, I had walked through a long, difficult season with a lack of privacy to deeply pray and heavy demands on my time as a wife and mother. One day I went to the bedroom to seek God for His guidance in this *narrow* place. As I went into prayer, I heard in my spirit, "In My Father's House are many mansions and if it were not so I would have told you." I stopped with a screeching halt in my prayers and asked the Lord, "Who is going to die?" I knew this was a passage of scripture often read at funerals. The Holy Spirit spoke with a commanding voice, "Get back into the flow of your prayer again; no one is going to die." Upon re-entry into my prayer, I had a sudden encounter with Heaven itself.

I do not know how the Lord does these things. I can only bear witness to what happened. I was *caught up* by the Spirit and was standing in the midst of my home in Heaven. I will try to describe what I saw. The walls were iridescent energy fields about a foot thick. The window openings were Spanish in design with a beautiful arch at the top, but there was no glass panes. The entrance to my home was a large archway opening, but no door was needed.

As I stood inside my home, I could hear music, but I did not see an electronic device to play a recording. I heard someone say, "In this place, you can tune music in or out as you choose. You may also go and join the choir or stay alone." There were pieces of furniture and on a table was fruit to eat. In an area to my right were a large window and a table with a lump of clay which was ready to mold into a piece of sculpture. This was covered with a large piece of cloth. There was an easel with a canvas ready to paint. I was told that I would be able to do artistic things I had wanted to do. Things I could not do well in the earth would be absolutely possible, because the Father is still Creator God.

I realized then what was not in my house. There were no clocks, telephones, radios or TV's. However, there was a small instrument I could compare to the size and design of a computer, with the ability to connect me to the King's Library, so that I could study and continue to learn what I had not learned during my lifetime on the earth.

Suddenly, I was escorted out of the house by an angel and walked down the street, past many other dwelling places to the River of Life. In this location, multitudes of people were having a wonderful time; swimming, picnicking and sharing in fellowship. The trees on either side of the river were full of bright green leaves and colorful fruit. I was not allowed to look to my far right, but I sensed the Throne of God was there.

Suddenly, the scene faded as quickly as it had come and I was back in my bedroom. Filled with amazement at this surprising encounter, I was so free, because I knew no matter how narrow, how long or how difficult the way was before me, one day what I had just seen would be mine forever.

This experience took the fear of death away from me completely, because Heaven had become a tangible reality. You may ask if it will look exactly like what I have described when we get there. I don't know, but my heart is assured that Heaven will be all we need and much more.

I can testify that in our day, altars are designated locations where God can show up. We all have places of divine encounter, because everyone has a life journey in which there is a love story to tell of God's faithful keeping power. There are so many ways the Lord will definitely reveal Himself during each person's journey.

There are times in just speaking about His grace that we are touched by the Holy Spirit and realize that the sweet presence of the Lord is close by. Our words of personal testimony are powerful in releasing hope and victory to others. When we share the tangible ways Jesus has touched us, protected us, provided for us or guided us through a hard place, then our words encourage others in their journey and strengthen us too. The Word says, "And they have overcome (conquered) him by means of the blood of the Lamb and by the utterance of their testimony..." (Revelation 12:11)

Joseph's altar—

The seed of Abraham multiplied through Jacob's twelve sons and one daughter. The one son upon whom I want to focus our thoughts is Jacob's favorite son Joseph, who was born in his older years out of his deep love for Rachel. Jacob's preference for Joseph created jealousy amongst the other brothers who seized him out in the field and threw him into a pit to destroy him. We can understand that pit quickly becoming an altar of prayer as Joseph cried out in the dark for God's mercy and help. (Genesis 37)

God answered that request, but mercy took on an unusual form and life was forever changed. There was a caravan passing by and the brothers chose to sell Joseph, sending him away on a difficult journey. Joseph continued to walk in the favor of God in spite of his hard circumstances and was successful in his position as a slave in Egypt. He caused his owner Potiphar to become more prosperous. Joseph was tempted by Potiphar's wife, but he rejected her and left her alone. She lied about him to her husband and Joseph was thrown into prison because of her scorn. Here too, in this dismal location, Joseph made an altar of prayer seeking God for rescue. (Genesis 39-41)

The Lord gave Joseph favor with the warden of the prison and he was put in charge of all the prisoners. Whatever Joseph did in this narrow place, he excelled, because the Lord was with him and made whatever he did to prosper. (Genesis 39:23) Yet we cannot help but wonder: How many times did he pray leaning against that damp, stone wall and cry for change and deliverance? Did he remember the dreams of his youth so long ago and question if God's promises would ever come to pass?

For all of us, life can hold difficult situations which can last extended seasons of time. Hardships and limitations can cause us to question God's faithfulness to us. This is when our own altars are so very important as we daily wait upon the Lord, seek Him diligently and anchor ourselves in the Word of God. In these hard, impossible places of the testing of our faith, we will come to a greater peace and deeper trust in God.

James wrote by the anointing of the Spirit:

> *Consider it wholly joyful, my brethren, whenever you are enveloped in or encounter trials of any sort or fall into various temptations.*

> *Be assured and understand that the trial and proving of your faith bring out endurance and steadfastness and patience.*

> *But let endurance and steadfastness and patience have full play and do a thorough work, so that you may be [people] perfectly and fully developed [with no defects], lacking in nothing.*

If any of you is deficient in wisdom let him ask of the giving God [Who gives] to everyone liberally and ungrudgingly, without reproaching or faultfinding, and it will be given him. (James 1:2-5)

Joseph had been cruelly forced to come into Egypt, but by God's grace Egypt did not come into him. In God's precise timing, the anointing of the Lord on Joseph's life brought him out of the dungeon to stand before Pharaoh. The leader of Egypt had received a dream and no one could answer his demands. When asked if he could interpret the dreams Pharaoh had received, Joseph boldly told the ruler it was not in him, that only God could give him a favorable answer of peace. (Genesis 41:16)

A gift of knowledge and words of wisdom were given to Joseph to speak before the court. The heart of Pharaoh was truly in the Lord's hand as he heard the interpretation of the dreams. Immediately, Joseph was given the highest rank possible and positioned next to Pharaoh. He would be used by God to save the nation and eventually rescue even his own family in a time of famine. All the years of hidden, difficult places of prayer and personal relationship with God ultimately positioned him for rulership.

Joseph, as Abraham's seed, had kept an altar in his heart from the pit to the prison to the palace. God used him to save thousands of lives in Egypt, see reconciliation with his brothers and bring his whole family to the land of Goshen. This is where Israel would dwell with favor and Abraham's seed would greatly multiply. When it came time for Joseph to die, he told his brethren that in the future God would visit them as a people and bring them out of Egypt and return them to the land promised to Abraham at his altar.

We witness the effect Abraham's faith and his altar building had as a covenant of God's favor upon his seed. Blessing after blessing came to the children of Israel because Abraham had chosen to be the friend of God. What will be the legacy and inheritance we pass on to our children and grandchildren? How will our current prayers and fellowship with the Lord be a covenant blessing for generations to come?

Please join with me in prayer:

Father God, We come to you with great thankfulness for all you have given. Teach us how to wait upon you until we are truly enveloped in your peace. Thank you for sustaining us through the hard places of life and granting courage to go forward by faith. We want to see not only our own deliverance, but the deliverance of our family and many more. Anoint us to pray for Your will to be done and for the nations to come to the knowledge of the Lord Jesus Christ. Help us to stand in agreement with your Word until Your answers come to pass. We are committed to follow You with our whole heart.

In Jesus's Name, Amen.

Considerations:

1. One of the truths I want to reinforce by writing this book is the need of a tangible altar in our living space, a specific location marked as God's place! This holy ground honors the Lord in a significant way and ushers in His Presence. This designated place declares your pursuit of God's heart. Deuteronomy 4:29, "But if from there you will seek (inquire for and require as necessity) the Lord your God, you will find Him if you [truly] seek Him with all your heart [and mind] and soul and life."

2. As we observe the lives of Jacob and Joseph, we are aware that it took many years to align them for their true destiny and purpose. The years of trial were a schooling period to educate these men in the character and ways of God. We see that eventually Jacob became Israel and Joseph became the provider for nations. Perhaps you have waited a long time to see the fullness of the Lord's promises in your life. He will not be one moment late in fulfilling His Word to you.

   Consider this thought with me: life is not about our circumstances or people's situations. Life is about our hearts and lives being changed through our right choices in Jesus Christ. When others look to you, do they actually see and sense Him?

   In Galatians 2:20, we find this statement, "I have been crucified with Christ [in Him I have shared His crucifixion]; it is no longer I who live, but Christ (the Messiah) lives in me; and the life I now live in the body I live by faith in (by adherence to and reliance on and complete trust in) the Son of God, Who loved me and gave Himself up for me."

3. One of the unforgettable scenes from Joseph's life is found in Genesis 45, when Joseph privately examined his brother's hearts to see if the years had brought change in their character. He then reveals who he is and forgives them freely. He does not rehearse the details of his painful journey, but instead declares it to ultimately be the work of God. Genesis 45:4-5, "And Joseph said to his brothers, Come near to me, I pray you. And they did so. And he said, I am Joseph your brother, whom you sold into Egypt! But now, do not be distressed *and* disheartened or vexed *and* angry with yourselves because you sold me here, for God sent me ahead of you to preserve life." May the Lord grant each of us the courage to let go of former things, walk with peace in the now and be free to complete the work given to us.

Notes

Chapter 5 — Altars in the Wilderness

Read Exodus 1-34

I believe we need to be avid students of God's Word, candidly exploring and absorbing the fullness of the things written for us. When we hold a Holy Bible in our hands, we hold a vast, Heaven-sent, blood-bought treasure waiting to be explored and possessed. It is my prayer that we would value our liberty to study His Word and honor His invitation to know Him. We are instructed by Paul in I Corinthians 10:1 that we are not to be ignorant of these things, but look at the fullness of the scriptures and learn from all that is recorded.

This continuous enlargement of knowledge is established in my own life at my early morning altar. I rejoice in my precious sanctuary and value each day's opportunity to encounter the Lord. Revelation from the Word enlarges my understanding, paints deeper levels of truth into my soul and increases my vision.

Years ago, I received some basic lessons in painting skills while living in Germany. I offer them for your consideration as a spiritual comparison to growing in the Word of God. In one season of our overseas assignment, I wanted to try something new and creative. I chose to take a painting class at the craft shop on Ramstein Air Force Base. After purchasing all the needed supplies of brushes, acrylic paints, a palette and a mounted canvas, I attended my first class with keen anticipation of what I would learn. After all, my father and brother were both wonderfully skilled professional artists; surely all I needed was some basic instruction.

In the first step towards my initial *masterpiece*, I was instructed to use a wide, one-inch brush and cover the canvas in a very thin layer of ochre paint. This formed a light yellowish coating and absorbed into the dry, stark white canvas material. This also neutralized the background, so that I might begin my picture. As the canvas dried, I had to make decisions concerning what I would create. Would it be a still life or a beautiful pasture scene with a green valley and mountains in the background? Choosing the valley scene, I had to narrow things down to the central focus of the painting. Would it be a German farm house or a lovely onion-domed chapel by a brook? The actual painting could begin by placing large brush strokes of blue sky and green grass. I placed my building in the chosen location, defined it and proceeded to add trees, bushes, clouds and other small details to my scene. When I stepped back and looked at my work, it still lacked enough dimension. Therefore, I returned to the canvas, decided the time of day and began to add appropriate shadowing. The last step was to apply small strokes of pure white light. My art work was not bad. I felt my newly acquired painting techniques were good, but my abilities and genuine talent in this field seemed limited. Selah!

A little disappointed in my efforts, I actually sought the Lord and asked Him (rather childishly) why members of my family could be brilliant in this area, yet I did not receive this creative gift in my DNA.

He tenderly consoled my heart by saying, "I have given you the gift to paint with words!" I thanked Him for my gift. Later, in His amazing love, He led me to try clay and ceramic art, where I excelled and created many pieces for my home and as gifts for friends and family. I had artistic abilities–I just had to find my niche.

I certainly learned many spiritual applications from my painting classes. I realized my life was a canvas, known and seen by all who were associated with me. What was the central focus? Where was the light? Where was the shadow? I honestly desired to have the painting of His Word upon the canvas of my heart and upon the testimony of my life. Three decades later, I'm still working on it! The Lord is faithful as He continues to take me through the processes of change into His image, as I dine daily at His table.

His special invitation to come and meet with Him is written boldly across the pages of the book of Exodus to the newly rescued nation of Israel. The Lord was in a process of taking thousands of slaves and forming a new nation. However, taking the people out of Egypt had not yet taken Egypt out of the people.

For centuries, they had been dominated and controlled by difficult taskmasters as they were forced to endure hard labor through their slavery under Pharaoh. They needed God's provision, healing, a new pattern of thinking, boundaries of protection, and sometimes strong correction. They followed Moses into new territory led by the pillar of fire by night and the cloud by day. What a picture those words paint!

Following the death of Joseph, we find the sons of Israel were fruitful, multiplied abundantly, became mighty in strength and filled the land. God's promises to his servant Abraham to bless his seed continued to be established. The people of Israel were allowed to continue in Goshen undisturbed until a new leader arose who did not know Joseph. (Exodus 1:8) When this new Pharaoh surveyed the conditions of his nation, he was afraid of the Israelites's growing strength. In order to limit their power, Pharaoh chose to place them under extreme, oppressive bondage and the seed of Abraham became slaves in Egypt. They were ordered with the power of cruel enforcement to build the cities, temples and palaces of Egypt. (Exodus 1:13-14) This was great hardship and struggle, yet the more they were afflicted, the more they increased. (Exodus 1:12)

The native Egyptians became more suspicious of the Israelites and their struggles deepened. Pharaoh went a step further and required that the Hebrew male babies be destroyed at birth, but the midwives feared God and would not obey his order. The Egyptian people were then ordered to destroy the baby boys by throwing them into the Nile River to drown. Just at the time when this cruelty rose to its height, the Lord intervened and sent a deliverer. It has been well said, "When men are contriving the ruin of the church, God is preparing for its salvation."[9]

The Lord sent a baby boy to some courageous parents named Amram and Jochebed, who were motivated by faith to protect their son's life from destruction. "[Prompted] by faith Moses, after his birth, was kept concealed for three months by his parents, because they saw how comely the child was; and they were not overawed and terrified by the king's decree." (Hebrews 11:23)

Jochebed was inspired to create a reed basket and place her son prayerfully within this fragile, floating cradle near the river bank. Her young daughter Miriam watched with vigilance to see what would happen to her baby brother when the daughter of Pharaoh and her servants came to bathe. She was excited to

---

[9] Matthew Henry's Commentary; Exodus, Chapter 11

witness that Moses was rescued and drawn out of the Nile waters by the daughter of Pharaoh, who pitied him and named him Moshe (Moses). Miriam came out of hiding and offered the princess the help of a Hebrew mother. Moses was delivered back to his mother's arms until he was old enough to be taken to the palace, where for 40 years Israel's future liberator was educated, trained as a royal son, and became a heralded general in the Egyptian army.

Hebrews 11:24 declares that when Moses became a great man in Pharaoh's court, he chose to stand with the Hebrews and share in their shame and oppression rather than remain in the palace. He was convinced that the Hebrews were God's people and, stirred by his faith, Moses stood strongly against injustice.

However, when Moses took things into his hands and killed an Egyptian overseer, he fled for his life and spent 40 years in the desert. At 80 years of age he was a shepherd watching the sheep, when he encountered the Angel of the Lord in a bush filled with fire, yet the bush was not consumed. Only when this unusual sight captured his full attention did he hear the voice of the Lord calling his name. Moses was reticent concerning his orders from the Lord, but he finally agreed to return to Egypt with God's help and liberate Israel from oppression.

The Lord sent ten plagues against the Egyptians to cause Pharaoh to let them go. The Lord had instructed Moses, "But every woman shall [insistently] solicit of her neighbor and of her that may be residing at her house, jewels and articles of silver and gold, and garments, which you shall put on your sons and daughters; and you shall strip the Egyptians [of belongings due to you]." (Exodus 3:22)

Following the ninth plague, the Lord gave the people favor, for they were not to leave the land without a blessing. The Hebrew women had never touched valuable jewelry or costly materials, much less possessed them. What joy must have flooded their hearts to embrace such treasures as they shared the exciting news with their families and friends. Women are women in any generation. Selah!

Following this spoiling of the Egyptians, one last plague would take the lives of the firstborn of Egypt, while all of Israel would be spared by eating the Passover lamb and placing its sacrificed blood upon the side posts and the door of their homes. They were instructed to be fully prepared and ready to leave, because Pharaoh would order them out of the country during the night hours.

The book of Exodus describes in much detail the nation of Israel's miraculous deliverance out of Egypt, their wilderness experiences and God's revelation of Himself to His chosen people. The Lord's Presence came to dwell in their camp through the faithfulness, prayers and obedience of His servant Moses. When the nation arrived at Mount Sinai and settled the camp, they took time to sanctify and prepare themselves for Divine encounter.

Moses went up to meet with the Lord at the mountain top and he came back to the camp bringing the plans of God to build a holy dwelling place for God's presence, which would be called a tabernacle. This portable tent for God's presence was to rest in the middle of their camp. Its tangible establishment invited men to meet with God through offerings and sacrifices at designated altars which were consecrated to the Lord's service. I have found that researching the details of the tabernacle grants vivid examples of redemption, fellowship, worship, communion, and even holy protocol.

We could truly fill many shelves of a library with the books and papers written concerning the experiences of Moses, Aaron and the tribes of Israel through the chapters of Exodus. However, the purpose of this chapter is to share how the altars raised up by these servants of the Lord became places of tangible encounter with the Living God.

The first altar along Israel's journey across the wilderness was built to shout victory over their enemies when the tribes of Israel defeated the Amalakites at Rephidim. Following the fierce battle, Moses raised an altar with thanksgiving to God as a symbol of the defeat of their enemies. He called this altar *The Lord is my Banner*. (Exodus 17:15)

We move on with them through the journey until we reach and establish camp at Mount Sinai. When the tribes of Israel arrived, Moses heard the Lord calling him to come up the mountain. In the recorded portion of their conversation, the Lord gave instruction for Israel's relationship with Him and His rulership over them. (Exodus 19:4-8) When Moses brought these requirements to the elders and the people, they agreed and declared all that the Lord had spoken they would do.

Moses reported back to the Lord and the people were instructed to sanctify themselves for three days. On the third day the Lord would powerfully descend upon Mount Sinai and Moses would enter the cloud of the presence of God on the mountain top. During this time on the mountain, the Lord gave Moses the Ten Commandments; ordinances for the people and directions for the construction of an altar.

> *An altar of earth you shall make to Me and sacrifice on it your burnt offerings and your peace offerings, your sheep and your oxen. In every place where I record My name and cause it to be remembered I will come to you and bless you. And if you will make Me an altar of stone, you shall not build it of hewn stone, for if you lift up a tool upon it you have polluted it. Neither shall you go up by steps to My altar, that your nakedness be not exposed upon it. (Exodus 20:24-26)*

I want to point out that these instructions came with a promise that "wherever He records His name, He will come and bless" those who worship there. This promise is as valid today as when it was received at Mount Sinai. Altars are still places of tangible presence and blessing. However, it is not enough to just build them; we must fill them with continuous worship, prayer and obedience. Altars are meant to be alive with His presence, not just beautiful in design or location. We can invite the Lord to write His name again in our heart, home, business and church fellowship that we, His people, may experience the fresh blessings of the Lord.

Years ago, I had the privilege of serving in a local church, where I headed up the prayer team ministry for the altar work of the church. The church decided to hold a series of revival services and one night during worship, the Lord gave me a brief vision. In the Spirit, I saw myself entering the sanctuary altar with the Lord. Jesus was carrying a large, wooden bucket of water. I walked beside Him and asked what He had come to do. He replied that the water He was carrying was for the people. I responded, "Lord, I want to see a river of water here, not just a bucket." He stopped and looked at me very seriously and said, "This people cannot have the river until they have humbled themselves to receive the bucket. I have come to wash their feet free of the things of the world." His answer overwhelmed my heart, as I was reminded that the Lord has not changed His mind about holiness and purity. He is merciful and gracious to forgive our sin, but He is also worthy to be served with great excellence and purity of heart.

Looking back at the beginning of this chapter, let us be reminded that we are painting a testimony known by God and vividly seen by others. If you are the only Christian canvas being seen by certain people, what is their vision of God?

The tribes of Israel had been raised in a heathen society, where many false gods were worshiped. In the Egyptian altars murder of human life, nakedness and sexual perversion had abounded. The Lord was teaching His new nation how to leave their slavery behind and come to His altar, where they could worship Him with freedom and purity.

In Exodus chapter 24, Moses recorded all the words of the Lord in a Book of the Covenant. He raised up an altar with twelve pillars to represent every tribe and offered blood sacrifices to seal Israel's new covenant with God. He returned to the mountain for 40 days to receive the Ten Commandments written on stone, the law with the instructions which he was to teach the people and the designed plans for a tent of meeting.

However, back in the camp, the people rebelled and raised a false altar in the form of a golden calf. The Lord wanted to destroy them all, but Moses travailed in prayer on their behalf as he asked the Lord to remember His covenant promises to Abraham and Isaac. Moses was allowed to come back down into the camp to bring judgment and correction. He was so furious when he saw their behavior, he shattered the commandments written by the Lord on the ground. All the Levites gathered to him with their swords and 3,000 men died that day.

In Chapter 34:1-3, the Lord called Moses back to the mountain with two freshly cut tables of stone and he made a new covenant with the people. After 40 days of being in the Lord's presence, Moses was allowed to descend the mountain with the stone tablets. It was time to bring forth the blueprints and build the tabernacle. This special tent of meeting would welcome God's presence and hold four Heaven-designed altars, plus the laver and the lampstand. The freewill offering, which was brought willingly by the people, would be used to create a glorious house for His presence. In Exodus, Chapter 25 to 31, the Lord had given to Moses all the instructions on how to design and create this dwelling place, which would display the Gospel message in type until the coming of Messiah, when Christ would fully pay with the shedding of His own blood the price for man's redemption. The study of the materials, measurements, and features of the tabernacle is the most written about subject in all the scriptures. I invite you to Exodua chapter 6 to look again at the strategic placement and worship function of the tabernacle furniture.

Please pray with me:

Father God, I ask you to stir our hearts with the truth that we are called and chosen to represent You and Your work in the Earth. We, too, are here for a strategic hour. Help us in this our day to be brave and faithful like Amram and Jochebed. May we experience the miraculous ways of the Lord and lead others to recognize and trust in the Living God. Help us to worship in purity of heart and be a beautiful painting in the Master's hands. Teach us how to enter into Your Presence and bless You with our faithful companionship. We love you, Lord God, and want to honor You with all that You have given to us. Our world is waiting to see us take the spoil of our battles and build something worthy of Your name!

May it be done, Amen.

Considerations:

1. Amram and Jochebed, the parents of Moses, were people of courageous faith and prayer. They rejected the murderous plan of Pharaoh and trusted God to have a way of escape to protect their son. Although they were slaves, the Lord used them to bring forth a deliverer, whom He educated in the palace courts, trained as a mighty general to later lead His people out of Egyptian bondage. We must never limit God...He can save by many or by few and His timing is perfect!

2. Perhaps at one time in your life you felt called to do something for the Lord, yet it never developed and you have laid it aside. I suggest you seek the Lord and ask if it is time to bring forth the vision and make it plain.

3. We must receive the washings of the Lord. The outpourings of the Holy Spirit are greatly needed in this dry land. The key is to humble ourselves before Him, seek His face and freely receive the Living Waters. I pray that you would receive a refreshing!

Notes

Notes

Chapter 6–The Tabernacle Altars

Exodus 25-40

Over my years of serving the Lord at altars of prayer, I have greatly enjoyed the study of the tabernacle altars. Each step of the journey, from the outer court to the Holy of Holies, has had immense significance to me personally. I pray that this chapter will communicate and bear witness with your heart also as we continue our journey with Moses and the tribes of Israel.

While the tribes of Israel were enslaved in Egypt, the Israelites were forced to build cities, tombs and palaces; but as they left Egypt behind and journeyed to the middle of nowhere, they were instructed by Yahweh to build a magnificent portable structure for His Presence to abide with them.. I have thought about the Lord's advance provision for this great building project in the wilderness. He caused the tribes of Israel to be fully prepared with gifts of gold, silver, jewels, fabric and polished mirrors gathered from the Egyptians before the Israelites left Egypt. Now the Lord requested His people to give of these treasures with a joyful heart to build Him a house in which to dwell amongst them. He told Moses, "Speak to the Israelites that they take for Me an offering. From every man who gives it willingly and ungrudgingly with his heart you shall take My offering." (Exodus 25:2)

Amazingly, the people were so generous, Moses had to ask them to stop giving because more than enough materials had been gathered for the project. I think many a leader has read these words of Holy Writ and longed to have the same situation!

In Exodus, we are given well defined descriptions of the six unique pieces of tabernacle furniture. Each piece was created to exactly agree with the pattern Moses had received from God. These furniture pieces were dedicated to the Lord's service and used only by consecrated priests. The priests were given specific procedures for blood sacrifices and washings to enter the Holy Place in the tabernacle tent, where they served daily at the altars of the Lord. Later it would be written in I John: 5:7, 8:

> *"So there are three witnesses [in heaven]: the Father, the Word and the Holy Spirit and these three are One; and there are three witnesses on the earth: the Spirit, the water, and the blood; and these three agree [are in unison; their testimony coincides]." (Psalm 95:2)*

Everything involved with the tabernacle was a witness and testimony to the Trinity.

I have enjoyed studying teachings on Tabernacle for many years. I recognize that the Lord's placement of the brazen altar, laver, lampstand, the shewbread table, altar of incense and the Ark of the Covenant form a cross. I find this positioning was symbolic in revealing the Gospel message and the ministry of Jesus Christ, which was taught by each piece of furniture.

I also believe the furniture can be a powerful pattern to use for personal prayer. As I used this in my own prayer life, I read some comments spoken by Dr. Paul Yongi Cho, who said that this layout of the furniture was his *personal jogging trail*. He would daily start at the brazen altar and begin his devotions by searching his own heart, declaring the blood of Christ was his sacrifice. He said that sometimes he felt the need to stay a long time at the brazen altar before moving on to the laver.

The metals used in the furniture were gold and brass; although, it would perhaps be a better translation to say copper or possibly bronze instead of brass. The lampstand was exquisitely designed out of pure gold and the laver was solid brass and amazingly made from the donated mirrors of the women. In the case of each of the other altars, the metal was placed over acacia wood, which is described as being incorruptible wood.

Let's examine some of the purposes of these altars and study them in the order in which they were crafted by the anointed artisan, Bezaleel. The Lord said, "I have filled him with the Spirit of God, in wisdom and ability, in understanding and intelligence and in knowledge and in all kinds of craftsmanship." (Exodus 31:3) Aholiab was inspired to help him and they were both anointed to teach other *wise hearted* men in whom God had placed wisdom and understanding to know how to do all the work.

Let's look at the furniture of the tabernacle in the order in which each piece was constructed:

1. The Ark of the Covenant

   a. The ark, which was constructed of acacia wood overlaid with gold, was located in the Holy of Holies. It represented the presence of God the Father.

   b. Upon the ark rested the mercy seat covered by the wings of two angels.

   c. Inside the ark was: a gold pot of manna which was God's daily miracle of provision;

   d. The rod of Aaron, which had budded proving the anointed authority of Moses and Aaron; and

   e. The tablets with the written commandments of God, revealing his justice.

   f. Only the high priest could enter the Holy of Holies once a year on the Day of Atonement. He came with the blood from the sin offering and incense.

   g. The ark was often taken into battles and went before Israel at the crossing of the Jordan River.

For a moment, I would like to consider why the ark of the covenant was the first piece of furniture the Father chose to have created. I think it shares a picture of the fullness of His heart towards mankind. The furniture project began with their focus on the Almighty God coming amongst them in mercy and benevolence. It demonstrated how much He desired to enter their midst and dwell with them.

The completed tabernacle area was created to welcome His presence and give Him a gracious place to abide with His people. The Holy of Holies, where the ark rested, was a hidden place of His power and within that ark, under the mercy seat, we find a declaration of His commandments, daily provision of manna, and the rod which budded and miraculously bore witness of His appointed leaders who walk in anointed authority to minister to the people. Over the ark was the covering of His holy angelic messengers who are sent forth to help the heirs of salvation. What a dramatic visual this inspires in our own hearts as we recognize the love, mercy and miracle provision of God to daily keep us as we maintain a relationship with Him. Behold the promise "Come close to God and He will come close to you..." (James 4:8)

2. The Shewbread Table

This table was in the holy place within the tent. Only the priests could enter this area daily to take care of the lampstand, the incense altar and bring the 12 loaves of freshly pierced bread every Sabbath. This ornate gold table held the shewbread, which means "the bread of my face" and was eaten only by the priests. This bread symbolized their reliance on God for their daily needs and provision. He not only wanted to be in their midst; He wanted communion and fellowship with them.

Today, the bread that rested on that table is symbolic of our daily provision and communion with God. We have been invited to fellowship with Him and with other believers through prayer, worship and the study of His Word. This is the promise of our communion table, where we take of the wine and the bread in remembrance of the suffering of Jesus Christ in His death on the cross. "The bread which we break, does it not mean [that in eating it] we participate in and share a fellowship (a communion) in the body of Christ?" (I Corinthians 10:16)

3. The Lampstand

This was the only source of natural light under the four layers of covering over the tabernacle structure. The lamp burned continuously before the Lord and was fueled by olive oil. The wicks were trimmed and kept clean morning and night to maintain the proper, pure light. The light was reflected brightly by the golden interior walls.

The Lord wants us to commune with Him and then be enlightened by the Word of God. This lamp represents the light of the Gospel, the illumination of the Holy Spirit, the knowledge of God's Word and our daily need to shine brightly in this world. The almond design is symbolic that the Lord will hasten to perform His Word. "I am alert and active, watching over My word to perform it." (Jeremiah 1:12) As we pray and study the Word, we are trimmed and prepared to burn brightly. Truly, the darker the situation, the brighter we can shine.

As a way of comparison, I remember going into the planetarium at the USAF Academy for a heavenly presentation of the stars. My eyes had to adjust as I came into the dimly lit room searching to find a seat to watch the performance. The show began and the room became even darker as the perimeter of lights at the ceiling faded and the stars became our only focus. As a part of the demonstration, they told us to sit very still as they removed even the stars in the ceiling and we were buried in a shroud of gross darkness. It was not a pleasant experience, but the moderator kept talking and eventually lit one small glowing light. In that pitch dark room, even one light was welcome and became the center of our attention. I was glad when the lights were brought up to a higher level. However, this demonstration made me think about how necessary our one light is in this dark world. Even the smallest light may be the only light for someone. May we shine!

4. Incense Altar

Uniquely made incense was burned twice a day on this altar at the same time the lamp was refilled and prepared. The incense altar was positioned directly in front of the ark of the covenant with only the thickness of the inner veil in-between. At this altar, the priests ministered to the Lord and blessed His name as they offered the incense and a significant fragrance rose up to fill the Holy Place and saturated the veil before the ark of the covenant.

All true worship is experienced by faith. Our worship increases as we come to know the Lord through daily communion and the study of His Word. Out of the abundance of our hearts, there should be a continuous flow of thanksgiving and praise to the Lord. (Psalm 95:2)

    1. *"Let us come before His presence with thanksgiving"*

    2. *"Let us make a joyful noise to Him with songs of praise."*

In Psalm 141:2 we find that *prayers* are like incense before the Lord. We read,

    3. *"Let my prayer be set forth before Thee like incense... " (Psalm 141:2)*

I always picture the incense altar as a place of great personal worship and earnest seeking after His heart directly before Him.

When we come into our places of private or corporate prayer, there is the necessity of heart *correction* and *connection*. All worship should be relational, interactive and full of faith or we can find ourselves trying to draw nigh with empty words and routines. We ourselves will be disappointed if we are not truly engaged at the heart level; but we will also disappoint the Lord because of His desire for our hearts to be one in Him.

Jesus prayed in John 17:-3

    And this is eternal life: [it means] to know (to perceive, recognize, become acquainted with, and understand) You, the only true and real God, and [likewise] to know Him, Jesus [as the] Christ (the Anointed One, the Messiah), whom You have sent.

Moving down to verses 20 and 21:

    Neither for these alone do I pray [it is not for their sake only that I make this request], but also for all those who will ever come to believe in (trust in, cling to, rely on) Me through their word and teaching,

    That they all may be one, [just] as You, Father, are in me and I in You, that they also may be one in us, so that the world may believe and be convinced that You have sent Me."

Brazen Altar of Sacrifice

This altar is the altar of *atonement*. We read that when it was time to set up the tabernacle and the brazen altar, the priests and this altar were anointed and then for seven days they were set aside symbolizing holy consecration. (Exodus 29: 35-37)

The altar of sacrifice was a place of judgment and amending of sin. The priest offered the blood sacrifice. The people came with their animals, realizing their need to be right with God. However, the blood of animals only covered their sin and pointed the way to the cross. It took the shed blood of Christ to deliver men from sin.

This is why we can easily visualize the brazen altar as the foot of the cross and the starting point of the Gospel. They are places to remember the cost of our salvation and experience His presence as our hearts are yielded with joy to the Master's touch.

6. Laver

The Laver is a brass basin shaped from the mirrors of the women and filled with water in order that the priests might wash their hands and feet before entering the Holy Place and before each sacrifice. This may have literally protected them from disease, but it was also a symbol of the washing of the Word, refreshing and baptism.

The Almighty God placed His seal of approval on the completed construction and ministry of the tabernacle. Standing at the gate for a full view of the tabernacle and its inner court, the presence of the Lord was visibly resting upon the tent. We read in Exodus 40: 34, "Then the cloud [the Shekinah, God's visible presence] covered the Tent of Meeting, and the glory of the Lord filled the tabernacle!"

We often hear people talking about touching or entering the glory. I still remember the first time I experienced the glory of the Lord. I was in a local church service and the altar had been opened for people to come and pray for a deeper experience. As a brand new Christian, I was hungry to truly know the Lord. I went down to the altar asking for something I could not explain in words, but my heart hungered to receive. Someone came over to stand with me in prayer and we sought God together. Suddenly, I saw a glorious, heavenly Light! It was filling my vision and my very being with the tangible Presence of the Holy Spirit. I had an encounter of the highest kind and those moments at the altar changed my life!

The Word says we can go from glory to glory in our walk with the Lord. He demonstrates Himself when and where He chooses and we are never the same. This is one of the reasons I have taught on altars for many years. I firmly believe they are places of divine encounter.

In studying all the tabernacle furniture, we can recognize and identify with the different aspects of the ministry of Jesus Christ. Our God is the Master Designer and Architect of the Universe. In considering His design for the tabernacle and meditating upon it as a *drawing nigh to Him*, I would like to present to you an opportunity for personal prayer possibilities.

Let's consider the step by step order of ministry in which these pieces of furniture were positioned and approached by the priest in the outer court, the Holy Place and the Holy of Holies. As we gaze upon this order of approaching God, we also see the work of the Cross.

Stand at the gate of the outer court with me for a moment and let's picture the scene:

1. Look at the blood-stained brazen altar
    Visualize this blood stained altar as the foot of the Cross, surrounded and secluded by pure white curtains

2. Move closer towards the tent and stop at the laver.
    Consider the washings and refreshing as we are preparing to enter His Presence

3. We enter the Holy Place and we are standing in the horizontal arm of the cross with the fullness of Christ's sacrifice and ministry.
    The lampstand, incense altar and the shewbread table.

4. In the Holy of Holies, we find angels guarding the presence of God the Father at the mercy seat. Even the contents of the ark of the covenant reveal to us what the Father has tangibly given to His people in authority, anointing, daily provision and written commands.

Here are some passages of scripture to consider as we ponder the pattern of the cross within the Tabernacle furniture and pray for understanding...

The Brazen Altar–Hebrews 9:14

> *How much more surely shall the blood of Christ, Who by virtue of [His] eternal Spirit [His own preexistent divine personality] has offered Himself as an unblemished sacrifice to God, purify our consciences from dead works and lifeless observances to serve the [ever] living God?*

The Laver–2 Corinthians 3:18

> *And all of us, as with unveiled face, [because we] continued to behold [in the Word of God] as in a mirror the glory of the Lord, are constantly being transfigured into His very own image in ever increasing splendor and from one degree of glory to another; [for this comes] from the Lord [Who is] the Spirit.*

James 1:22-24 (Amplified Bible)

> But be doers of the Word [obey the message], and not merely listeners to it, betraying yourselves [into deception by reasoning contrary to the Truth]. *For if anyone only listens to the Word without obeying it and being a doer of it, he is like a man who looks carefully at his [own] natural face in a mirror; For he thoughtfully observes himself, and then goes off and promptly forgets what he was like.*

The Lampstand–Ephesians 1:17-19

> *[For I always pray to] the God of our Lord Jesus Christ, the Father of glory, that He may grant you a spirit of wisdom and revelation [of insight into mysteries and secrets] in the [deep and intimate] knowledge of Him,*

By having the eyes of your heart flooded with light, so that you can know and understand the hope to which He has called you, and how rich is His glorious inheritance in the saints (His set-apart ones),

And [so that you can know and understand] what is the immeasurable and unlimited and surpassing greatness of His power in and for us who believe, as demonstrated in the working of His mighty strength.

The Shewbread Table–John 6:35

Jesus replied, I am the Bread of Life. He who comes to Me will never be hungry, and he who believes in and cleaves to and trusts in and relies on Me will never thirst any more (at any time).

I Corinthians 10:16-17

The cup of blessing [of wine at the Lord's Supper] upon which we ask [God's] blessing, does it not mean [that in drinking it] we participate in and share a fellowship (a communion) in the blood of Christ (the Messiah)? The bread which we break, does it not mean [that in eating it] we participate in and share a fellowship (a communion) in the body of Christ?

For we [no matter how] numerous we are, are one body, because we all partake of the one Bread [the One Whom the communion bread represents].21

The Altar of Incense–Psalm 25:14

The secret [of the sweet, satisfying companionship] of the Lord have they who fear (revere and worship) Him and He will show them His covenant and reveal to them its [deep, inner] meaning.

The veil has been removed and every believer is invited to walk boldly past the outer court and into the Holy Place. We are recipients of the Light, participants at the communion table and active worshipers of our God. There we stand before the ark of the covenant and freely celebrate our blood-bought relationship with our heavenly Father. Somebody ought to shout, "Yes, Lord!"

Please pray with me:

Father, we thank you and stand in awe of Who you are and what you prepared from the foundation of the world in giving us your Son. We worship from the altar of our own hearts with praise. You are our amazing God! Please continue to teach and guide us through the Word as we learn how to raise up our personal altar and come into Your presence to be one with You. We are grateful Your invitation to us is always, "Come and learn of me." We truly want to learn; therefore, we stand on Your Word found in Matthew 11:29. "Take My yoke upon you and learn of Me for I am gentle (meek) and humble (lowly) in heart, and you will find rest (relief and ease and refreshment and recreation and blessed quiet) for your souls." Amen, Lord, so let it be.

Considerations:

1. The Tabernacle is very relevant for us today, because it so reveals Jesus Christ. The fellowship that the Lord desired to have with His people then is the same fellowship He desires today. We come through the perfect sacrifice of Jesus Christ. God truly made us for Himself and His eye is ever upon us. The Tabernacle was at the center of the camp, so all could come and worship. Will we let God tabernacle in the center of our lives?

2. The table of shewbread brought the priests into weekly communion with God. Our altar of prayer should also birth communion with God. I made the decision several years ago to take communion daily in remembrance of the victorious work of the Cross and with a declaration of the Lord's power to heal and sustain my life. It is not a ritual but a personal connection to the victorious work of the cross.

3. I pray that you would take the time to consider these altars again recognizing the importance of each table and location. God is so awesome in His details. This tabernacle altar pattern still makes an amazing walk of prayer.

Notes

Notes

Chapter 7- The Altars of His Generals

Isaiah 55:4

Behold, I have given him for a witness to the people, a leader and commander to the people.

In studying the unique and holy altars Moses had crafted in the book of Exodus, we have considered the descriptions and worship functions of the furniture found in the tent of meeting. The tabernacle was created in the wilderness by divine design using the tangible spoil gathered out of Egypt. The tabernacle was furnished with tables of service and altars, which welcomed the Lord's presence and demonstrated to the tribes of Israel how they were to approach a Holy God as Jehovah chose to dwell amongst them.

When Moses made his request for materials, the people had donated the expensive things they had brought from Egypt with joy as a freewill offering in order to fully accomplish all the planned design and construction of the tabernacle. The Lord released anointing upon designated artisans who would create all of the intricate designs and exact patterns. Every piece was completed, delivered and set in its proper position according to the detailed blueprints Moses had received on Mount Sinai. Moses thoroughly inspected all of the work and then blessed those who had labored so diligently to meet the high standards of the Lord. (Exodus 39:43) Once all things were completed, the Lord required a special day of consecration in order to bring every altar and priest before the Lord in holy dedication. (Exodus 40:1-15)

Such vivid, tangible worship symbols cause me to remember the deep reverential fear that invaded my own soul when I first came to know the Lord. I had come out of darkness into His marvelous Light, and by that illumination the reality of His Holiness was written on my heart. In that season of experiencing new life in Christ, I was reminded that a deep respect for the Lord, for prayer and for His house had always been in my heart. Even as a young child when someone would pray, I would stop, close my eyes and bow my head until they said *Amen*. As a teenager living in a small southern town, I often walked several blocks by myself on Sunday mornings to enter the closest local church near my home.

One summer, the church I attended sponsored a young people's retreat weekend and I went with the group, not knowing what to expect. In the large living room of the lake retreat center on that first evening, the leaders dimmed the lights as guitars began to play worship music. I still vividly remember a picture of Christ hanging over an altar table with the bright glow of a nearby candle flame flickering across the image of His face. During those moments, His image drew my heart like a magnet as the Lord conveyed the reality of His presence to me. He was so alive! His tangibility was engraved in my heart and mind to such a depth that it remains alive 50 years later! I will be eternally grateful that, by His grace, He inscribed on my heart an understanding that He is to be honored, revered and respected.

We have been looking at altars for six chapters and observing the lives of those who built altars in the book of Genesis. We have seen how an altar gave revelation and increased their relationship with God. I pray that the value and true merit of having a personal daily altar has become more important to each one of us through these studies. From my own experience, I know I would not have made it through some of the seasons of my life if I had not maintained my altar and a journal of my walk of faith. These have helped me to encourage myself in the Lord like God's general, King David, when he stood alone in the desolation of Ziklag! (I Samuel 30:6) The Lord is truly able to redeem our difficulties and turn our ashes into victory if we will dare to believe and worship! Now let's consider some other generals in the faith.

His General—Joshua

During the weeks the tabernacle tent was being prepared and established, we read that Moses set up a separate tent outside the camp where he would go and meet with God on a daily basis. Moses did not go to this tent alone, for the scripture states that he was accompanied by Joshua, who had become an aide to God's servant. (Exodus 3:1) When Moses would return to the camp, Joshua would remain by the tent guarding the entry, and he would tarry in the presence of the Lord. Through his service to Moses, he had encountered the Great I AM and nothing compared to fellowship with Him.

From the beginning of the 40 year journey across the wilderness, Joshua had proved himself faithful, steadfast and courageous. When he was sent to spy out the land of Canaan, he and Caleb came back with the good report that the Lord was certainly able to give them the land. The tribes of Israel refused to believe their report. As the book of Exodus ends, Joshua and Caleb are the only survivors who came up out of Egyptian slavery. In the refining process of the 40 year journey, Joshua had become Israel's top general and Moses was instructed by the Lord to name Joshua the next leader of His people. Through his faithful service Joshua had been "tested and groomed" to lead the nation into the Promised Land. A faithful general to replace God's servant Moses had faithfully come up through the ranks.

Exiting the book of Exodus and entering Joshua 1, we hear Jehovah's direct charge to Joshua with His promises of success if Israel would observe the commands of the Lord. Wherever Israel stepped, God would step and give them possession of the land! Sounds awesome! It *was* awesome! However, it certainly came with a touch of fear, because their new walk and transition into the land would require a greater faith and the risk of their own lives in battle. Therefore, the Lord said repeatedly, "Joshua, be strong and of good courage." (Joshua 1:9)

In times of transition or difficulty, we need to hear and declare by faith the comforting strength of God's Words again and again. It is important to focus on what we have been given through Jesus Christ. One method of increasing our faith is to make declarations from the scriptures. Write down verses on small cards and place them where they are easily read every day. As we read them out loud, our faith is increased, the peace of God comes and the reality of Truth builds up our confidence. We have received the promise that, "faith cometh by hearing, and hearing by the word of God." (Romans 10:17) As I mentioned in an earlier chapter, we are told in Jude 20, "Beloved, build yourselves up [founded] on your most holy faith make progress, rise like an edifice higher and higher], praying in the Holy Spirit." (Jude 20) There is proven power in agreement and we need others to be in prayer with us. We must conquer our reservations, doubts and fears as we seize the opportunity to turn what looks like defeat into a mighty victory, and then we are at liberty to walk in our destiny! Amen.

We can sometimes feel that the Lord is building the bridge across the difficulty even as we step by faith, and not one moment before! I counsel you to keep walking straight forward in cadence with the Lord! As we advance, we need to mark those special places of victory to remind us how God led us through many days of change.

We can thank God for the anointed leadership He provides through the inspiration of His people. On the other side of the Jordan, the people had pledged themselves to Joshua's leadership, "All you command us we will do, and wherever you send us we will go." (Joshua 1:16) When Israel faced the churning waters and then miraculously crossed the Jordan on dry land, Joshua immediately obeyed the Lord's instruction and marked the location with a stone of memorial for each tribe. (Joshua 4:7) This was a tangible witness to generations yet to come to reverence and fear the Lord. These stones "cried out" a testimony to all people that the Lord our God is great and mighty! Do you ever wonder what kind of legacy your faithful walk with God is leaving to generations yet unborn?

Joshua led the people into the Land and onward through many God-given victories. When the city of Ai was taken, Joshua was grateful for the faithfulness of God and he raised up an altar to the Lord on Mount Ebal. Joshua also inscribed on those altar stones a copy of the law of Moses. He declared the words of the Lord before all the people as they began to follow him into the land. (Joshua 8:30-35)

Scenes like this remind us of our own need to write down the victories of our lives and the faithfulness of God along life's journey. We, too, need to declare the Word of the Lord, write down words of thanksgiving and raise up altars of remembrance, lest we forget His goodness. Throughout many years of serving the Lord, my daily journals have been a source of personal strength and a reminder of how the Lord guided and kept me along the way. There is something about writing things down that makes the experience more tangible. I can go back over those anointed pages and read them again to encourage and exhort myself. Years ago, I came across the prayer journal which belonged to my husband's grandmother. She was a dedicated Christian and her love for the Lord and prayers of concern for the souls of her family members was absolutely inspiring.

During Joshua's lifetime, the Promised Land was apportioned section by section to the different tribes and the tent of meeting was raised up as an altar for the nation. "And the whole congregation of the Israelites assembled at Shiloh and set up the Tent of Meeting there; and the land was subdued before them." (Joshua 18:1) Later, just before his death at 110 years of age, Joshua called all the people to meet with him and declared to them that they must choose whom they would serve. He declared that he and his family had made their choice and they would serve the Lord. (Joshua 24:15)

There is a great need in our day for every believer to come to such a place of total commitment and consecration to the Lord. This requires a private altar relationship with consistent study, prayer and worship. We do not work *for* God and simply do good things. We learn by personal interaction how to yield and work *with* God, "For we are fellow workmen (joint promoters, laborers together) with and for God; you are God's garden and vineyard and field under cultivation, [you are] God's building. (I Corinthians 3:8-10) Joshua had learned by faith and following! The pattern has not changed. The church has far too much restless activity instead of being yoked with Christ, abiding in Him and moving when He moves! (Matthew 11:28,29) What a liberty it is to just follow the Head of the Church!

Along this line of thought, Judson Cornwall gives us this interesting analogy,

> "Assuming you have been a successful applicant for a job, would you prefer to hear on your first day of employment: "Here's a book of instructions, and there is the equipment. Follow the instructions and you will soon catch on," or: "Here, join me. You'll learn as we go along. I'll give you personal on-the-job training"—which? Assuming that the boss is a pleasant individual, certainly you would prefer to work *with* him than merely *for* him. No one knows better what needs to be done, when it should be done, or how to do it than the boss."[10]

The message of faith and servanthood was in Joshua from Egypt, through the wilderness, to the altars of tabernacle and on into the Promised Land with altars of victory, corporate worship and total family unity. From altar to altar, the Lord had indeed strengthened him to become courageous and a great leader of his people.

His General—Gideon

A general in the making is found in the 6th chapter of the book of Judges. When we first come upon Gideon, we find a frustrated man hiding in the darkness of a cave, as he endeavored to thresh some wheat for his family. In this passage, we are viewing a strategic moment as Gideon receives a visitation from the Angel of the Lord.

Amazingly, the Angel promptly greets Gideon as a mighty man of fearless courage and states that the Lord is with him. Immediately, Gideon's response is a flood of serious questions, as he asks why the enemy has the power to strip Israel. Where is the God Who delivered them in former times? While he is mumbling and grumbling about the condition of his nation and the hardships of his people, the Angel totally ignores Gideon's frustration and shares instead an amazing statement in Judges 6:14, "The Lord turned to him and said, Go in this your might, and you shall save Israel from the hand of Midian. Have I not sent you?" (Judges 6:14)

Because of his personal turmoil and negative attitude, Gideon cannot grasp this direct command from the Lord and begins to give excuses of how this could not possibly be the truth. Did you ever tell God how wrong He was about a certain matter? How often our negative confessions shut down our ability to walk in faith and hear divine plans and creative possibilities.

When I began my journey with the Lord and our family began to attend a local church, I was asked by our Young Adult Sunday School teacher to teach our class in her absence. My reaction was like Gideon's, "Who, me? Surely you do not understand my inabilities." I did not even pray about it; I just said, "No!"

In a few weeks, the opportunity was presented to me again and I felt a deep conviction in my heart, but my fear of public speaking overwhelmed all other feelings and I said, "No," for the second time. However, my teacher's request for help would not leave my mind and when I got home I prayed and truly sought the Lord. I gave Him every excuse why it was impossible, yet I had no peace. Suddenly, I had an idea and presented my proposal to the Lord. I told Him I did not want to say *no* to Him, because He had done everything for me and I loved Him. Yet because of my fears and lack of understanding in the Word, I asked if

---

[10] Let Us Abide, Judson Cornwall, p.68

He would allow me to start with teaching little children and work my way up. I promised I would never say *no* to Him again! I could almost hear the Lord chuckle and say, "Gotcha, Elaine."

In my mind, I felt what I had proposed would take years of preparation and service, but I would study and be faithful to my promise. In the many functions of the running of our local church, there were needs; first, in the nursery, then it was time for VBS and I was given a room full of rowdy little boys who actually listened to me. Next, the teen class had a real need and I was asked to substitute teach for several weeks, and at the same time the young girls needed a leader, so I began to work with them. Over a period of barely six months, I taught in these various levels and suddenly, one Sunday morning, I saw our Young Adult Sunday School teacher headed my way again. As my eyes riveted on her, I knew in my heart that God had established this moment. For the third time, I was asked to teach the class and I realized I had to keep my promise to God and answer the call. I said a very shaky but definite, "Yes!"

I earnestly studied the teaching guide and my Bible, fasted and prayed for that Sunday morning class. I can still remember how nervous I was as I stood grasping a podium in front of that small group of people. However, when I began to teach I felt the presence of the Lord and the anointing of God came upon me. It was as though I stepped over to the corner of the room and the Lord took over and spoke through me to the hearts of those present. I was forever changed, because there is nothing that compares to obedience and the anointing of the Lord. What a privilege it is to share the Gospel and witness the faithfulness of the Holy Spirit touching lives. Truly, that morning the Lord ruined me for the ordinary and placed a deep passion in my heart for the extraordinary things of a life lived for Him.

Centuries before me, Gideon had an encounter of the highest kind in the 6th chapter of Judges and it forever changed his life and the lives of many more. He brought an offering of food to the Angel of the Lord and it was consumed by fire from the Angel's staff. At that moment, the fear of the Lord hit Gideon as he perceived that he had been in the presence of God. The Lord mercifully promised Gideon that he would live through this divine encounter and not die. Gideon immediately established his first altar of worship which he named "The Lord is Peace." (Judges 6:24) When the Lord's power and glory are truly revealed to us, we are forever changed and it will cause us to raise up a place of remembrance where we may honor Him.

That very night, the Lord commanded Gideon to go immediately, destroy the false altars of his father and raise up the true altar of the Lord. The altars of idolatry in the land were the very reason Israel was in such bondage to the enemy. The Angel of the Lord had boldly questioned the nation of Israel in Judges 2:2, "And you shall make no covenant with the inhabitants of this land; but you shall break down their altars. But you have not obeyed My voice. Why have you done this?" False altars were the hindering force and the source of their affliction.

The Lord was looking for a man who would tear down the false altars and establish a fresh covenant with the Living God. Gideon realized that his obedience to this command could mean the loss of his family and possibly even his own life, but his fresh encounter with the Lord and his fear of God gave him faith and courage to obey. Concerning this command of the Lord, Matthew Henry makes these observations:

> "See the power of God's grace, that he could raise up a reformer; and the kindness of his grace, that he would raise up a deliverer, out of the family of a leader in idolatry. Gideon must not think it enough not to worship at that altar; he must throw it down and offer

sacrifice on another. It was needful he should make peace with God, before he made war on Midian. Till sin be pardoned through the great Sacrifice, no good is to be expected."[11]

Because he was afraid of his Father's wrath and the hostility of the people of the city, Gideon waited until nightfall to gather ten servants who would go with him to perform the word of the Lord. They took his father's seven-year-old bull and went to the false altars of Baal and Asherah in the grove of trees. His orders were to pull down Baal but chop down Asherah. Then in the midst of this stronghold of idolatry, he was to set stones in proper order, raise up a pure altar and use the remains of Asherah as kindling wood on which he offered his father's bull as a blood sacrifice to the Lord. When the darkness of that one night passed, a new day would dawn on Israel and a general was birthed for the nation's defense.

The next morning, the men of the town wanted to kill Gideon, but his father would not turn him over to their vile ways. Out of Gideon's obedience, the Lord had caused his father to stand with him and not against him. It is a powerful thing to have the blessing of our heavenly Father as well as our earthly father.

Immediately after these things, the enemy rose up in unity to invade and destroy Israel. We read in verse 34, "But the Spirit of the Lord clothed Gideon with Himself and took possession of him, and he blew a trumpet, and [the clan of] Abiezer was gathered to him." The Lord began to lead His new general from one victory to another, empowered by the anointing of the Holy Spirit to bring His people to freedom and a turning back to the true altar of the Lord. I think Gideon was probably more surprised than anyone else in Israel that the Lord chose him to become His general to lead the nation and defeat the enemy.

E. Stanley Jones wrote in his book *Abundant Living*:

> "What must we do to accomplish the works of God? John 6:29 says, 'Jesus replied, This is the work (service) that God asks of you: that you believe in the One Whom He has sent [that you cleave to, trust, rely on, and have faith in His Messenger].' When I am believing, then I am really working, for then I become a channel of the Infinite. When we are surrendered to God we can do what we can't—we find ourselves miracles to ourselves."[12]

Out of our personal encounters with God and our yielding to His purposes, how many more people will be set free by Truth, inspired to know Him and embraced by peace? May we emerge out of our personal altars where our tears for the souls of men and nations have been, as Spurgeon said, "liquid prayers before our Lord." Let us be clothed with the same Holy Spirit as Gideon. May we be equipped by the Spirit to be bold in our obedience by night or by day, to tear down the hindering things of darkness and raise up the holy things of the Lord. This is the work of intercession and comes only out of tangible relationship. Only the Lord knows how much can be changed for good if we are obedient to seek His face and follow on to know the Lord in this desperate hour of national and international need!

Please pray with me:

Father, we want to come out of our fear-filled caves—we come to you asking forgiveness for our mumbling and grumbling. May we stand up for Truth, receive Your gift of faith and be freed from the opinions of men (including our own doubts) as we perceive and follow the guidance of the Lord. We ask that we might have

---

[11] Matthew Henry's Concise Commentary

[12] Abundant Living, E. Stanley Jones, p.107

a fresh encounter with Your glorious Presence. We want to be a people of courage and service to You and then touch our fellow man. We take authority over our fears and ask for renewed purpose to arise in our hearts. We ask for leadership to come forth through Your Word and the inspiration of Your Spirit. May we bring down the obstacles and false ways of our generation and build upon the solid Rock, Christ Jesus. In His Name we pray, Amen.

Considerations:

1. Do you remember your first encounter with the Lord? That moment when He revealed Himself to your heart and somehow you knew He loved you. Whatever your experience, that was a life-changing, eternity-birthing moment. We need to stir up our remembrances of His presence and keep Him alive in our daily experience. The scriptures warn us to not forget our first love. Revelation 2:4, *"But I have this [one charge to make] against you: that you have left (abandoned) the love that you had at first [you have deserted Me, your first love]."* Take time to focus, remember and recapture the precious presence of God. It is recorded in Mark 12:30 that Jesus said, *"And you shall love the Lord your God out of* and *with your whole heart and out of* and *with all your soul (your life) and out of* and *with all your mind (with your faculty of thought and your moral understanding) and out of* and *with all your strength. This is the first and principal commandment.*

2. We have witnessed in this chapter that the Lord has His own way of preparing His generals for leadership. He equipped and anointed them for their positions. They in turn believed, trusted, followed and faithfully obeyed Him. How is the Lord preparing you? His schooling can seem hard at times, but He alone knows what it will take to strengthen us to reach our destiny. Never give up, never lose sight of Him, rest in His care. His chosen ways will be perfect for you and usher you into greater understanding and deeper fellowship with Him. Our goal is not a ministry — our goal is to know Him and serve Him well.

Notes

Notes

Chapter 8— The Altars of His Kings

Psalm 24:3-5

Who shall go up into the mountain of the Lord? Or who shall stand in His Holy Place? He who has clean hands and a pure heart, who has not lifted himself up to falsehood or to what is false, nor sworn deceitfully? He shall receive blessing from the Lord and righteousness from the God of his salvation.

Our invitation to *Come and Dine with the King* continues as we turn the pages of Old Testament scripture to consider the altars of three prominent kings of Israel: King Saul, King David and King Solomon. Each one of these monarchs was anointed and appointed by God to rule, guide and protect their nation. They walked in high moments of great victory, but as rulers they also made wrong choices which caused these kings and their people to suffer terrible consequences. I believe we can understand more about the *spiritual etiquette* of altars by observing the way these kings approached them.

Entering the first book of Samuel, we find the judges of Israel and the strength of the priest's office has begun to fade away as the leadership of the prophets comes into position. In the first few chapters of I Samuel, we witness the importance of prayer, travail, perseverance and obedience to the commands of the Lord. Altars had a definite impact on the transition of the entire nation.

Chapters 1 and 2 of I Samuel reveal Hannah's endurance and earnest prayers for a child as she sought God at the altar in Shiloh. In God's timing, she received more than her highest hopes. The Lord blessed her with *an anointed son for the nation,*[13] whom she named Samuel, and as time passed by the Lord surprised her with five more children. We will share more of her testimony in Chapter 10.

In chapter 2, we find Hannah's son Samuel was dedicated to the Lord and left to be trained at Shiloh. He was a young boy living in the residence of Eli the High Priest. One night, Samuel was awakened repeatedly as he heard for the first time the voice and instruction of God. After that experience, the Lord appeared to him and revealed Himself to Samuel as he encountered His Word in Shiloh. (I Samuel 3:21) The scriptures make the bold declaration that when he grew to manhood "*... the Lord was with him and let none of his words fall to the ground.*" (I Samuel 3:19) He was born to be a prophet and became an altar builder, intercessor, teacher and the mouthpiece of God to his nation. Each of Samuel's altars was a place of divine encounter, instruction, protection and great victory for Israel.

Later when Samuel was getting older, he appointed his sons to be judges. (I Samuel 8:1-5) However, this did not work out because of the grievous sins of his sons. Then the people of Israel decided they wanted to

---

[13] NIV Study Bible, P. 482

be like the other nations and all of Israel came to the prophet Samuel asking for a king. He greatly resisted their suggestions and demands. He brought his grief-filled prayers to the Lord. After waiting on the Lord, he was instructed to tell the people they had rejected God. Through a series of events, the Lord proved to Samuel that He had chosen Saul to become the king. As the Lord's scribe, Samuel wrote in a book the manner in which the kingdom was to now operate in relationship with God and the new king. Their new king had boundaries and was not appointed to be an absolute ruler; rather he was to be subject to the laws of God and the words of the prophets. Thus the people were given their desire to transition to a king; however, the Lord was to remain the ultimate Sovereign Ruler of the nation.

There are seasons of transition for every living thing and this truth extends globally. However, times of change can only be bridged by earnest prayer, understanding of needs and receiving the counsel of God. I often compare such transition to the well-known visual of the London Bridge in London, England. This span of concrete and steel begins with watchtowers and ends with watchtowers. I think this visual represents a powerful analogy of how to manage transition. The watchtowers of unified prayer protect the entry points and the journey across the bridge. Then the unity of prayer creates a safe, stable entry on the other side so that the transition is handled well.

Looking at the current transitions of my own country, I often consider that America was birthed as a nation of great liberty and opportunity because our forefathers came with a Bible in their hands and a personal relationship with God in their hearts. They had the wisdom to seek out and raise up altars of prayer, both privately and publicly. They knew that freedom could not be obtained nor maintained without the Word of the Living God granting us His Wisdom and Leadership. In Exodus 33:15 and 16, Moses received from the Lord the transitional instructions for the tribes of Israel. We find these words, "And Moses said to the Lord, If Your Presence does not go with me, do not carry us up from here! For by what shall it be known that I and Your people have found favor in Your sight? Is it not in Your going with us so that we are distinguished, I and Your people, from all the other people upon the face of the earth?"

In these difficult, changing times, altars of prayer for America's healing and freedom are once again desperately needed. Instead of being overwhelmed, we can dedicate ourselves to prayer, be aware of what is happening in current events, pray for leadership, vote our convictions and stand up in faith for justice to be established. The Lord has promised in II Chronicles 7:14, "If My people, who are called by My Name, shall humble themselves, pray, seek, crave, and require of necessity My Face and turn from their wicked ways, then will I hear from heaven, forgive their sin, and heal their land." We can choose these actions as individuals, plus gain strength by gathering with others of like heart to seek the Lord.

In my own life, I have personally experienced many seasons of *crossing over* and transition. It can be uncomfortable, challenging, even misunderstood by those closest to you and it can be financially expensive to make the move. However, the Lord told me at the beginning of my journey as a new believer to never put roots down so deep that when He said, "Go," I would not go. During the weeks or months of being uprooted and replanted, I found maintaining my altar of prayer, journaling my daily feelings and meditating on the scriptures in my private times with the Lord kept me steady, secure and headed in the right direction. At best our knowledge is limited, but our God is all-knowing. We are not our own, but bought with a price; therefore we are His. We can trust Him, the King of the Universe, with our present and our future. He really does have a plan for every life and is able to perform it. If we will choose Him above all else, then His plans will be revealed and His Way known. This in no way means that every move I have taken would have been my personal choice or preference. However, it does mean I have learned that He knows what is best for me and I can trust my life to His care.

Perhaps you have noticed that when it is God's time for transition, you can sense something is about to change because you begin to feel like you are surrounded by a glass box. I call it the *glass house syndrome*. You can see and you can hear but you are no longer a part of the surroundings. There is a feeling of being disconnected, even though you are still there physically and maintaining the same routine of daily living. You realize something else is formulating which has not yet become tangible. In some ways, I have come to understand that this *glass house* is the protection of the Lord over our hearts in order that we may leave the old with genuine peace when the time comes to move on.

In such seasons, it is very important to wait upon the Lord until we know we are being led forward and not driven by some circumstance or emotion. We must also realize that others may not have a clue to this time of transition and that's okay. In the changing seasons of life, be careful to wait quietly on the Lord in faith, without inviting the opinions of others until things are coming together with form and substance. When something tangible has begun to form, then your transition will make more sense to you and to others. You can share your considerations and pray about it corporately with those who really care about you as a person.

In a time of transition, the tribes of Israel wanted a king and Saul was selected by the casting of lots to come out of the tribe of Benjamin and take center stage. (I Samuel 10:20-23) Saul entered the position, demonstrating humility. Then the anointing of the Lord came mightily upon him to rally the people to war and God gave them victory. (I Samuel 11:6-8)

After a two year period, the Philistines rose up against Israel. The king called the army to join him in Gilgal. The army was fearful, and as several days went by Saul refused to wait any longer for Samuel to come and offer the sacrifices. Saul was the king, but he was not called to be a priest. He deliberately determined his independence from God's established order. In great disobedience to God and in fear of the enemy, he took it upon himself to go to the altar and offer the burnt offerings, which he was forbidden to do. (I Samuel 13:9) When Samuel arrived and found out what Saul had done, he announced that the kingdom was taken from Saul and would be given to another man whose heart was one with the Lord. (I Samuel 13-14) This was King Saul's *altar of pride and presumption* birthed out of fear. He did not trust the Lord or the prophet Samuel to come on time. The condition of King Saul's heart ripped the kingdom from his grasp.

Later, Samuel died and the Philistines came up to fight against Israel again. The Lord refused to answer King Saul's request for guidance and Saul went another step in his rebellion, as he searched out a witch to find an answer by familiar spirits. At this *forbidden altar*, Saul was told he would lose the battle, the kingdom, his own life and his sons. We find an important statement in Deuteronomy 30:19: "I have set before you life and death, the blessings and the curses; therefore choose life, that you and your descendants may live."(Deuteronomy 30:19) Saul had chosen death in this final act of disobedience.

How do these events affect us today? I fully realize and rejoice in the truth that we do not live under the law, but under grace. Our sacrifice is the work of the Cross and our callings and anointing come by the power of the shed blood of Christ. Jesus did not come just to forgive our sins; He came to remove the power of the sin nature within our hearts so we could live in freedom and righteousness. That being truth, doesn't it make sense that in our approach to daily walking with the Lord in private worship or public ministry and service, we need to be very aware that even this side of the Cross, we can grieve the Holy Spirit by our prideful ways of deliberate disobedience and our failure to recognize God's holiness? May we always approach the Lord, His work and His altar with faith, humility, purity, love and respect. Truly,

I believe the Lord is still looking for those who will live by faith and passionately pursue His heart, not merely ask for things from His hand!

We know that David was such a man with a heart after God, because the Lord declared it was true. (I Samuel 13:14) Yet we wrestle with the facts found in the scriptures that David was a murderer and guilty of adultery. He was quick to repent, but he suffered in the deep personal losses his sins ushered into his life and nation. His mistakes cost the lives of others, including the life of his firstborn by Bathsheba. We find King David came to an altar of mourning because of his bad choices in that tragic series of events. (II Samuel 12:16)

When David was waiting to be positioned for the throne, there was the provision of an *altar which fed and equipped him.* (I Samuel 21:3-9) At a moment of danger prior to becoming king, David was helped by Jonathan to flee from King Saul's jealousy. David went to the priest at Nob and the altar of the Lord for support. At David's personal request of the priest, he was given five loaves of holy bread right off the altar of shewbread to sustain his life. He was also given the massive sword of Goliath with which to fight. I am sure David well remembered the day the Lord had given him the strength to swing that sword against Goliath's neck to defeat the enemies of Israel.

As we read the Psalms, we find some insight and realize that David was an anointed worship warrior who spent long hours from his youngest days worshipping God. As the king of Israel, he publicly demonstrated his heart for God by vigorously dancing before the ark of the covenant as the altar was brought into Jerusalem.(II Samuel 6:14) He faithfully established the Tabernacle of David and set the Levites singing the praises of God continuously. This is the altar where he worshipped, fasted and prayed. He who held a throne knew how to touch the Throne of God.

I have found there is greater edification and revelation from the Lord when we establish a strategic place of prayer in our homes. There is a release of our faith to receive His Presence when we meet with God in a certain chair, at a private table or even sitting quietly on the floor at the end of our bed focused on Him. For me, this becomes holy ground and a place of magnified breakthrough. The Lord is invited to minister to me there, we converse together and the place becomes saturated with the Holy Spirit. What a comfort this is in hard times. What a joy it is in our daily experience to know God with us! I understand King David's need for hallowed ground and a designated place which became a point of contact with the Almighty! Truly, such a chosen position has kept my life and maintained my soul.

David earnestly wanted to build a permanent house for the Lord in Jerusalem. He gathered the materials and drew the plans for this magnificent structure. He shared his heart with his son Solomon, who had been chosen by the Lord to rule the nation with wisdom and build the temple in Jerusalem.(II Chronicles 25:5,6) The Lord would have His dwelling place amongst His people.

Later, King Solomon gathered the people of Israel in unity to offer 1,000 sacrifices to the Lord at the bronze altar made by Bezaleel in the wilderness. That evening, the Lord appeared to Solomon and asked what he wanted to receive. Solomon requested wisdom and knowledge to rule the Lord's people. (I Chronicles 1:10) He was granted his request and the Lord added riches, honor and glory like no king had ever possessed. He was now prepared to rule the people and build the house of the Lord, which would be the symbol of God's presence amongst His people and a witness to all nations that they should fear the name of the Lord. God promised Solomon that His eyes would be open, His ears attentive, and His heart present to hear the prayers offered in this set apart place, which He had chosen and sanctified. (II Chronicles 7:15,16)

In my own experience, a designated place with a prayer altar which has been made holy by God's presence is still an invitation to the eyes, ears and heart of God to come to us as believers and teach us His ways. In the day to day living of our natural lives, it is imperative to have tables where we may eat, study, and share together. The same thing is true in the spirit, as we come to the Lord's Table to fellowship with Him. This creates a place of encounter and exchange with Him! It is such glorious news that we are not just His servants, but also His friends. We do not have to wait for Heaven to know the Lord. We have been invited to dine with the King and kiss the face of God!

King Solomon had a brilliant start and he continued to build cities and gain possessions. In the beginning years of his reign, the Lord called Solomon *Jedidiah* (beloved of the Lord), but Solomon began to defiantly love many foreign women. The Lord had commanded Israel not to mingle with these women, because such relationships turned the hearts of men to the false altars of their nations and this undermined the foundation of the society. Solomon built temples to their deities and joined in their worship. Solomon's heart became divided, as he did evil in the sight of the Lord and did not fully follow God as his father David had done. (I Kings 11:2,6) His failure to keep God first and the sin of his divided allegiance ushered in a tidal wave of false worship, which caused the whole nation of Israel to be rent in half after his death.

We can easily comprehend from the study of these kings that the altar where we serve and how we serve the Lord at that altar are important factors, not only for our own souls, but for the sake of others who will be impacted by our choices now and even into the generations which follow. We often influence others more than we realize and we, too, are influenced strongly by what is around us. Judson Cornwall wrote in his book *Things We Adore*: "Association, commerce, culture, education and training stand out in my mind as powerful contributors to idolatry—both for the Hebrews and for modern society."[14] The voices around us in our day to day living can greatly influence our hearts. It would be wise to consider who and what is influencing us and whom are we influencing. A good way to check and know what we adore would be to consider where and with whom we desire to spend our time and our money.

This might be a good time to prayerfully evaluate our hearts. David cried out to the Lord and said, "Search me [thoroughly], O God, and know my heart! Try me and know my thoughts!" (Psalm 139:23)

Please pray with me:

Father God, as we consider the worship of these kings of Israel, we come with humility asking You to search and reveal our hearts to us. Renew a right spirit within us; empower us again by Your love to worship with pure hearts, for we are only refreshed in Your Presence. We ask for healed, pure hearts free of divided allegiances, pride, stubbornness and deception. May we wait upon You by faith with expectancy and perseverance. Enable our prayers to be as fervent as Hannah's as we choose to establish room for You in our daily lives and invite You to invade our private territory! Above all, we ask to be known in the courts of Heaven and in the Earth as the friend of God. Thank you for your open door policy and unending faithfulness to us. In Jesus Name, Amen.

---

[14] Things We Adore, Judson Cornwall, Page 30

Considerations:

1. Have you experienced the "glass house syndrome" and wondered what was happening? I truly believe it is the Lord's way of covering our hearts and preparing us to change. If you find yourself in transition, remember the Lord knows the end from the beginning and is in charge of all the changes. Trust and be not afraid. He will be right on time to take you forward.

2. God promised Solomon that His eyes would be open, His ears attentive, and His heart present to hear the prayers offered in this set apart place, which He had chosen and sanctified. (II Chronicles 7:15, 16) We, too, are the temple of the Lord; therefore may I suggest to you that this is still true of our places of worship and prayer. We are not alone, for God is with us and watches over His Word to perform it. In everything and through all situations, lift your needs to Him and make your requests known. Place all things before Him and know He will supply even over and above what you have asked.

3. Remember that King Saul and King Solomon both had a brilliant start. But when they began to walk in pride and worship other gods, they marred their destiny and hindered the things of God. Let us guard our hearts with all diligence and stay humble before the Lord. May His blessings rest upon you and take you fully into your destiny.

Notes

Notes

Chapter 9— The Altars of His Prophets

Revelation 19:10

Worship God! For the substance (essence) of the truth revealed by Jesus is the spirit of all prophecy [the vital breath, the inspiration of all inspired preaching and interpretation of the divine will and purpose, including both mine and yours].

In previous chapters, we have observed altars being used by the Lord's generals and kings. In this chapter, we will go further into the scriptures and study the altars of some of His prophets. Their Spirit-anointed prophesies established truth and justice in their generations.

At the beginning of Chapter 8, we mentioned the life of Samuel and we noted that his mother brought him forth by travailing prayer. Hannah established the early days of Samuel's life as she fully obeyed the vow she had made to the Lord. Samuel was a prophet, altar builder, intercessor, teacher and the voice of God to his nation. We stated that his altars were places of divine encounter, instruction, protection and brought great victory to Israel.

Samuel was trained by Eli the priest from early childhood to minister directly to the Lord. As he matured, Samuel was able to hear, receive and act on the Word of the Lord. Because of his ear to hear and his heart to respond to the Lord, God continued to visit the altar at Shiloh. (I Samuel 3:21)

While making these observations, I want to consider the importance of one faithful, righteous man or woman of God today. Just one person can make a difference and even take part in moving a nation back to God. May we never underestimate the important influence of one believer who has learned how to seek the Lord with the desire to be that *ear to hear* His Voice. Let us walk in covenant relationship to represent Him in a real world.

During Samuel's lifetime, the nation of Israel drifted away from the Lord, raised up their false altars, lost a battle with the Philistines and the ark of the covenant was stolen by the enemy. The Philistines placed the ark in their temple by their god Dagon. The statue of Dagon fell over twice due to the presence of the ark of the Lord, while disease and affliction came for seven months upon the cities of the Philistines. (I Samuel 5-6) The people were struck with such a degree of suffering that they begged their leaders to send the ark back to Israel. When the ark was supernaturally returned, it was received with joy in the fields of Beth-Shemesh. However, many men died that day because they looked into the ark without proper reverence for the Lord. Struck with fear, the people asked for the ark to be moved and it was taken to the house of Abinadab. Eleazar, his son, was established as a priest to serve at the altar. (I Samuel 7:1)

Twenty years passed before the people of Israel began to truly see their need and cry out to the Lord. They called upon Samuel, who required them to destroy their false altars and come to the Lord with a whole heart. They took action on his requirements and removed their idols. Returning to Samuel, they confessed their sins against the Lord, fasted and symbolically poured out a water offering of cleansing and renewal for the nation. Immediately, the enemy tried to attack them, but God's servant Samuel raised up an altar, offered a blood sacrifice and cried out to the Lord. The Lord promptly answered with a great voice of thunder and the enemy was scattered, thrown into confusion and defeated. (I Samuel 7:10) Samuel raised up a stone pillar as a permanent marker of their victory and named it Ebenezer (*which means stone of help*) as he declared, "Heretofore the Lord has helped us." Samuel's altars of worship and his obedience to God caused his life to become a marker which inspired and kept the nation.

Do we have any markers of tangible victory in our lives? Has our devotion to the Lord left an imprint of Him on other people? Is it said of us, "You have been with Him"? Victorious markers need to be recorded! I believe in keeping a daily journal, a continuous record of our daily walk, because it helps to establish definite dates and times when the Lord was especially leading us by His grace. It can be so encouraging to go back over our recorded personal exploits and witness again how the Lord faithfully led and supported us through situations.

One marked victory in my life happened at Panama City Beach, Florida. We were living temporarily at our beach property. The family was away during the day and I had purposed to spend five mornings straight in fasting and prayer as I was seeking the Lord for a deeper prayer life.

The first day was pretty normal with personal Bible study, worship and earnest prayer. Later in the day, I was surprised by a Christian program with inspired teaching on prayer. I thanked the Lord for His timing and looked forward to daily enjoying this special broadcast. The way God orchestrates such things for us simply proves Who He is!

The second day after my time with the Lord, I went outside to throw away the trash. We had not landscaped the yard yet, therefore all we had was beautiful white sand. I looked down as I descended the porch steps and saw a four inch wide mark pressed in the sand. It was a definite trail left by a large snake. I stopped to audibly pray and boldly declared the promises of God as my protection. After a few moments, I felt at peace that the snake had simply passed through the property and moved on.

The third day after my prayer time, I planned to run errands and go grocery shopping. I needed to go to the outside shed in the backyard to get an ice cooler. As I was about to cross the yard on my way to the small metal building, I saw a new snake track and was strongly impressed to stand still, take authority and pray.

I got still and heard the Lord say, "Follow the trail!" Reluctantly, I obeyed and found the trail went to the outside building I needed to enter. At the entrance to the shed was a large circular impression in the sand; this visual let me know a large snake had nested there during the night. Where was it now? Good question! The Spirit of the Lord instructed me to open the shed door and get my cooler. I hesitated, because I was afraid to obey His directive. My mind wanted to race with fearful thoughts and imaginations. What if the snake had crawled inside? I was totally isolated without neighbors or family. There was absolutely no one around to help me if I got in trouble.

I was told again to unlock the door and open the shed. Praying and obeying, I took the shed key placed it into the lock and threw the shed door open. I jumped back and looked carefully into the shed space.

All appeared clear and my heart stopped beating so fast as I took out the cooler with thanksgiving and relocked the shed door.

At that point, it was necessary for me to walk past my front porch to place the cooler by the fence gate near my car. As I walked slowly towards the front of the property, I saw that the snake track led away from the shed and went under the front porch deck. I stood still with the ice chest in my hand and wondered if the snake had come in, gone out or was it still there? I mustered the courage to go towards the gate, as I kept praying every step of the way, deposited my cooler by the gate and quickly walked around to the back door to re-enter the house. Safely inside, I prayed until I was at peace and truly calm in my spirit. I filled my arms with the things I would need the rest of the day, set the security system and hastily went out the front door, locking it behind me. I turned to walk across the porch and step down off the deck to go to the gate. I was startled when I saw a large snake head lying on the front door mat at the top of the porch steps. I did not hesitate. I immediately turned, opened the front door and returned to the safety of my living room. I turned off the security alarm, placed my things on the couch and came back to look at the snake head from the safe position of a glass door!

Moments earlier, I had walked past the front porch deck with my cooler. I had seen nothing. How had this large snake head been placed on the mat? I was physically shaking and asking the Lord a zillion questions, but I heard no answer. When I calmed down, I heard Him ask me, "What is the purpose of your prayer and fasting this week?"

I replied, "Teach me to pray!"

He responded with one word: "Well?" I went back in my mind over the experience of being alone and isolated, seeing the trail of a possibly dangerous enemy, praying, declaring the Word of God as my safety, obeying His instructions and conquering my own fear. I stood amazed at the Holy Spirit's vivid classroom instruction!

Now that moments had passed I felt a greater assurance, I had the courage to open the front door to see the snake closer. In spite of my shakiness, I was curious about how it died and I was looking for marks on the two inches of body still attached to the head. I was also looking around the porch for the rest of the body. The Spirit of the Lord arrested me and told me not to get too close to the snake head. I stopped moving and knelt down about three feet from the snake, looking right into his eyes. He was so recently torn from his body, his eyes *looked back*. He was still alive! I truly believed an angel of the Lord had separated the head from the body, rescued me and deposited the trophy of prayer where I could not fail to see it. Talk about a *victory marker*! May the Lord be praised for His mighty acts and His glorious, tangible reality. Amen, Lord!

In the book of Kings we find the prophet Elijah, who stood before the presence of God and spoke the judgment of God to King Ahab. (I Kings 18:15) Elijah declared a drought upon the nation and fled for his life to a brook called Cherith which was east of the Jordan. He drank the water and was fed by the ravens both bread and meat every day. Then over time the brook dried up and Elijah was given the instruction to transition over to Zarephath to wait in the home of a widow and her son until the time of the famine was totally ended. (I Kings 17:3-15)

The Lord instructed Elijah to go and stand before Ahab so that the rains might return to the nation and the drought be ended. Elijah searched for King Ahab and instructed him to gather all of Israel and all of the prophets of Baal and Asherah to meet with Elijah on Mt. Carmel. They would establish their altars and see who answered their prayers by fire. The false prophets had no results following hours of worshipping their gods. Then Elijah told the people of Israel to come close and observe as he took twelve stones representing the tribes of Israel and rebuilt the altar of the Lord which Jezebel had torn down. He dug a trench and then placed the wood in order and cut the bull in pieces, laying all the sacrifice out on the wood. He instructed others to take four jars of water and pour it over the wood and sacrifice three times. Now he had reached the exact timing of the evening sacrifice. He cried out for God to reveal Himself and bring the hearts of the people back to the Living God by answering his prayer and sending fire upon the altar. Immediately, fire fell from heaven and consumed every part of the altar. The people fell on their faces and cried out, "The Lord, He is God."

We live many centuries later, but we too can establish our altars of prayer and cry out for the fires of God to fall once again from heaven. We were recently on an Eagle Conference Call when the Spirit of the Lord revealed a large belch of fire coming out of Hell to invade the Earth. I saw a plague released upon the people. The next day the Spirit spoke to me again and said, "Cry out for the fire of God to come from heaven and destroy this work of the enemy. The fire of His altar is greater!" I remembered the description of Elijah on Mt. Carmel and prayed, "O Lord, display Yourself again. Send fire from your altar and bring our nation to its knees crying, *The Lord, He is God!*"

Now let's turn the pages of scripture forward and view another marker of God's presence, this time in the life of the prophet Isaiah. He saw the Lord and realized his personal sin and the sin of his people. Isaiah cried out and a coal was taken off the altar in Heaven by an angel and brought to touch Isaiah's mouth, cleansing him of all sin. Immediately, Isaiah could perceive in the Spirit and heard his instruction to go to the people of Israel and declare the words of the Lord. He received that call and was given exact orders from the Lord on how to speak with the people. This vivid altar experience of a heavenly kind was a time of personal cleansing, dedication and a launching into prophetic ministry for Isaiah. (Isaiah 6:1-10)

Personal encounters with the Lord change us forever as we answer His call. Truly the Lord stands at the door of our heart and knocks. When we open that door He will express Himself in His own perfect way for our lives. He will challenge us as He challenged Isaiah, asking, "Who will go for us?" I pray that each person who ever reads this book will attain their destiny in God. There is a promise of His guidance in Isaiah 48:17, "Thus says the Lord, your Redeemer, the Holy One of Israel: I am the Lord your God, Who teaches you to profit, Who leads you in the way that you should go." Amen, may it be so!

The prophet Jeremiah also encountered the word of the Lord and by faith embraced the call of God. He questioned his ability to serve, but he was assured by the Lord that he was chosen and ordained to be a prophet to the nation. The Lord put forth His hand and touched Jeremiah's mouth with the words of God and that tangible transaction was the marker that changed Jeremiah's life. From that time of spiritual encounter, Jeremiah heard the voice of the Lord clearly in words of strong prophecy for the nation. He was able to rise in divine strength which no power of the enemy could overthrow. (Jeremiah 1:18) Jeremiah endured hardships, rebellious people, confinement in the court of the king's guards, beatings, being locked in the dungeon and cast into a pit for speaking the Word of the Lord. These hard places became his personal altars and the markings of the Lord stood true. The word of the Lord was fulfilled through his life, even from a pit!

The Word of the Lord and revelation of His glory came to the prophet Ezekiel by the Chebar River. (Ezekiel 1) This scene from Heaven and the presence of God were so powerful, it took the Spirit of God entering into Ezekiel to raise him to his feet. Ezekiel was called and sent by the Lord to speak to a rebellious people. The Lord compared them to thorns, briars, and scorpions. (Ezekiel 2:6) In his encounters with the Lord, he was strengthened and instructed by many prophetic acts to tangibly demonstrate to Israel the things the Lord would perform amongst His people.

Later, Ezekiel was taken in a vision to watch the exact measuring of the sanctuary of the Lord in Jerusalem. There the Shekinah glory came and the Lord declared this would be where His feet would stand. Jerusalem would be the place of His rulership in the future and there would be an altar like the brazen altar, not to cover sin but to declare to all generations the price of our salvation by the blood of Jesus Christ.[15]

Let's look at other captives taken from Jerusalem. The prophet Daniel and three other young men were brought from Judah into the Babylonian palace as potential candidates to be taught the knowledge and language of the Chaldeans. They would be educated for three years and then be brought before the king for his approval. Daniel determined in his own heart that he would not defile himself with the food from the king's table and he requested that they could have a simple diet of grains and vegetables for ten days and prove they could remain healthy and strong. This was done and on all four young men the Lord poured out a blessing of knowledge, skill and wisdom; plus, Daniel had the anointed ability to interpret dreams and visions. Every table is considered an altar and Daniel chose to not defile their table.

There was a change of power and the new king, Darius, established three presidents over 120 princes and these men ruled over the kingdom. Daniel was the first president and some of the other men became jealous of him. Since they could find no fault with Daniel, they observed his daily prayer life and created a scheme to kill him. They caused the new king to sign a law that for thirty days no one could petition any god or man except the king. If they did, they would be thrown into the lion's den to be eaten alive. Daniel knew what had been written into law, but he still continued to kneel by his open window altar to pray and worship God three times a day.

The report of his prayers was brought to King Darius, who sought a way to protect Daniel, but he could not change the law. The prophet of God was cast into the lion's den as the king declared that God would protect Daniel. The king fasted all night and could not sleep. The dawn found him going hastily to the lion's den and calling out to Daniel, who answered that he was well because the Lord had sent His angel to shut the mouths of the lions. The king removed Daniel from the den and had the men who had tried to kill Daniel thrown to the lions. When we set our face to pray and serve the Lord, He will deliver us from the jaws of the enemy and the plots of the wicked.

In the Minor Prophets, we find false altars had corrupted Israel. There was the harsh reality of their faithlessness, yet the cry to return and be restored with the promise that one day there would be restoration. The people were unfaithful and without true knowledge of God from personal experience. (Hosea 4:1) The Lord described them as unfaithful and without appreciation. (Hosea 5:4) For them, their altars had become a place for sin (Hosea 8:11), yet the Lord asked them to return to Him in repentance and be healed. In Joel there was a plague and the cry of the prophet was, "return to God's altar." (Joel 2:15,18) That cry is being heard today. May we help many to come to true altars of worship and come to a right understanding of the Lord.

---

[15] The Dake Annotated Reference Bible, Page 1428, Column 1, a.

Let's consider for a moment the prophet Jonah, who had the most incredible altar in the belly of a great fish. He had received the word of the Lord instructing him to go to Nineveh to proclaim to the people that they needed to repent for their wickedness. Jonah did not want to obey the Lord and tried to escape by sea to another country. However, a great storm and Jonah's confession that he was running away from God caused the crew to throw Jonah overboard into the turbulent waters. He was promptly swallowed by a great fish prepared by God for His prophet. In this dark, wet, smelly place Jonah finally sought God with all his heart and cried out for help. The Lord spoke to the fish and it vomited Jonah out upon the dry land so he could continue his journey to Nineveh.

I have often considered God's great mercy on His run away prophet as there were only two ways of escape from that great fish. This is an amazing picture of deliverance and the mercy of God. I have wondered if Jonah's skin or hair was bleached by the chemicals in the fish's stomach. If so, he would have been quite a sight walking into the city and proclaiming the message of God. Jonah obeyed the Lord and went on to Nineveh. The king, along with all of his people, repented and even their livestock had to fast, as the people earnestly sought forgiveness. Jonah was very angry and pouted over God's mercy towards this people. (Jonah 4:1) The Lord told him there were 120,000 children in that city and many animals who had not sinned. God's mercy and grace far exceeds our own.

As we have observed the prophets of God, we have seen a strong, intricate pattern of sacrifice, service, obedience, courage, leadership and devotion to God. In closing this chapter, I want to share a portion of scripture by which I have been greatly encouraged. I have declared it as a prophetic word over my own life. I invite you to do the same. This passage is a portion of a prophetic prayer found in Habakkuk 3:17-19. We are told these words are set to wild, enthusiastic, and triumphal music:

"Though the fig tree does not blossom and there is no fruit on the vines, [though] the product of the olive fails and the fields yield no food, though the flock is cut off from the fold and there are no cattle in the stalls, Yet I will rejoice in the Lord; I will exult in the [victorious] God of my salvation! The Lord God is my Strength, my personal bravery, and my invincible army; He makes my feet like hinds' feet and will make me to walk [not to stand still in terror, but to walk] and make [spiritual] progress upon my high places [of trouble, suffering, or responsibility]!"

Please pray with me:

Father God, we come to the King of the Universe and humble ourselves before You in the name of Jesus. We have witnessed your faithfulness to protect, empower, and use your servants to be Your voice in the nations. We are not all prophets, but we can know and speak your Word in faith, for we are witnesses of Your grace. We thank you for your plans and purposes for our lives and our world. We pray for bold, Godly leadership to arise all over the Earth and take their positions of governmental authority in the nations just like the prophet Daniel. Grant us courage to speak, ears to hear your instructions, eyes of vision and the strategy of the Lord to plan and develop Your purposes. May we make definite progress with tangible results and hold fast to the joy of our salvation.

In the name of Jesus Christ we pray, Amen.

Considerations:

1. The prophet Samuel was a man who left a legacy of accurately hearing God's voice, building altars and establishing victory markers to testify of God's faithfulness. What kind of testimony will we leave for others? Our consistent walk with God becomes a *marker* to help others to trust and follow the Lord. May our words be like Samuel's and never fall to the ground. Paul encouraged Timothy in I Timothy 1:18-19

    This charge and admonition I commit in trust to you, Timothy, my son, in accordance with prophetic intimations which I formerly received concerning you, so that inspired and aided by them you may wage the good warfare, [19] Holding fast to faith (that leaning of the entire human personality on God in absolute trust and confidence) and having a good (clear) conscience.

2. The prophets of the Old Testament heard the word of the Lord, responded and acted upon it. I believe the Holy Spirit still speaks through His prophets to encourage and exhort the body of Christ. The scripture says in Revelation 19:10, "For the substance (essence) of the truth revealed by Jesus is the spirit of all prophecy [the vital breath, the inspiration of all inspired preaching and interpretation of the divine will and purpose, including both mine and yours]."

3. I Corinthians chapters 12-14 give us much instruction concerning the vital ministry of the Holy Spirit. The very center of those chapters is the love of God. Paul boldly states, "And if I have prophetic powers (the gift of interpreting the divine will and purpose), and understand all the secret truths *and* mysteries and possess all knowledge, and if I have [sufficient] faith so that I can remove mountains, but have not love (God's love in me) I am nothing (a useless nobody)." Prophecy should convey God's heart, exhort and encourage His people.

Notes

Chapter 10 — The Altars of His Handmaidens

Psalm 68:11

The Lord gives the word [of power]; the women who bear and publish [the news] are a great host.

Over the years, the bold witness of a host of women in the scriptures has strengthened my faith and encouraged me to persevere in prayer and service to God. We can all learn from the actions and responses of these brave women: Rebekah, Jochabed, Deborah, Jael, Ruth, Abigail, the widow of Zarapheth, the Shunammite woman, Martha, Mary, Joanna, Lydia, Dorcas and Priscilla.

In studying the scriptures for this chapter, I researched the lives of several women of prayer. After some consideration, I felt we really must start with Eve in the book of Genesis. It is recorded that in the beginning she knew God, walked with God and conversed with God daily. (Genesis 2-3) What amazing privileges of fellowship she experienced in those days of innocence. However, in Genesis 3, deception and sin brought a great separation from God's daily presence. Adam and Eve were cast out of the garden into a cursed, thorny earth. Their way was hard, but God's grace allowed the establishment of an altar for blood sacrifice and the first couple had the privilege of limited relationship with their Creator.

Reading further into Genesis, we witness that most of the recorded prayers by the wives of the patriarchs were earnest petitions beseeching the Lord for children. Rachael especially pleaded and wrestled with God for children. (Genesis 30:22) The Lord heard her cry and she received two sons.

Moving forward in time, we see Miriam (the sister of Aaron and Moses), who led the women of Israel in worship and was called a prophetess. Later, Deborah in Judges 4 was a prophetess, judge, and a valiant woman of God going to battle with Israel's armies at the request of their generals. I considered Queen Esther, who fasted with her handmaidens and risked her life in the king's court to save her people. The Lord gave her a bold strategy to expose the enemy to the king; her courage and timing released the deliverance needed and the tyrant Haman was hung on his own gallows. Esther's fervent faith is still celebrated around the world during Purim.

There are also the hidden handmaidens who pop up for a few brief verses in the scriptures. These ladies were recorded for all time by the Holy Spirit as women who prayed; their passionate cries touched God and brought Divine intervention and change. For instance, we find this to be true in II Kings 5, where we find a slave girl from Israel testifying to her mistress of God's power to heal and deliver through His prophet Elisha. Her master Naaman, commander of the Syrian army, dared to believe her faith-filled declarations and found his deliverance by obeying the command of the prophet with seven dips in the Jordan River. Following his healing, he took the dirt from that region home with him and created an altar of remembrance and thanksgiving, where he would continuously honor God for his healing.

I place the testimony of Hannah at the top of my list of the Lord's handmaidens. We have mentioned her in chapters eight and nine as the interceding mother of the prophet Samuel. Come with me as we revisit chapters one and two in I Samuel. I want to turn our gaze upon Hannah's passionate intercession during her long trial of waiting.

Over many years of ministry, I have had the privilege of sharing the pain, endurance and victory of these chapters with the Lord's daughters across the USA, in Bulgaria, India and New Zealand. In every nation, the women could easily relate to the longings of Hannah's heart and her desperate cry for personal victory. Being female is a gift from God and not a curse, but developing into a capable woman of courage and perseverance like Hannah is the faithful work of the Holy Spirit through a surrendered, prayerful life.

Hannah was married to a man of faith named Elkanah and the Word says in chapter 1, verse 5 that he loved Hannah and did everything he could to provide for her. He took his family, which included a second wife with children, to the feast at Shiloh year by year to worship the Lord. During the celebration the second wife, Peninnah, would deliberately speak out in a cutting fashion to hurt and embarrass Hannah. The only thing Hannah could eat was her own tears. Therefore, leaving her bewildered husband at the table, she ran to the tent and cried out to the Lord with all her heart. I have often admired her courage, because it would have been so easy in her womanhood to just run away to some isolated place instead of running to the tent of meeting to pour out her soul at the altar of the Lord. In an hour of such wrenching pain, we want to fight or flee, but by God's strength and grace we can flow. Hannah made the right choice to continue to intercede and it paid off big dividends for her, for a whole nation and for all generations since that time. She had no idea the future scope of God's answer to her prayers.

As she prayed at the tent, the place of God's altar, there she made a vow that if she was granted a son, he would be dedicated to the Lord's service. She was oblivious to the fact that Eli the priest was watching her and he was imagining she was drunk. Misinterpreting her actions, he came over at this moment of her severe pain and strongly corrected Hannah. She could have resented or run away from his words, but instead she explained with respect for his office the truth of her situation and her desperate need for God's help. I believe the Lord touched Eli's heart in that moment of time and he immediately declared, "Go in peace, and may the God of Israel grant your petition which you have asked of Him." (I Samuel 1:17)

There was a definite spiritual exchange at the door of the Lord's house in Shiloh, because we witness a believing Hannah arise; all sadness left her face and she ate a meal. She went back to her home rejoicing in God's faithfulness and the Lord remembered her with a baby boy. After she kept her vow to return little Samuel to the service of the Lord, she was granted a greater fulfillment of her heart's desire for children. The Lord faithfully blessed her womb with five more children. For this praying handmaiden of the Lord, her prayers were answered far beyond her request. She had sought the Lord for a son, but the Lord desired to bring forth a prophet for the nation. This would be a son faithful to Him as an inspired intercessor and bold leader.

For us, too, there can come moments of spiritual receptivity after long endurance in a difficult situation. There are times when we are graciously given a gift of faith to dare to believe God. There comes such a witness in our spirit that we know that we know our petition is answered and will come to pass. Such a faith-filled moment manifested in my life after our son David was born. When he was a seven months old, David began to develop nickel-sized red whelps on his body. I took him to the doctor and they ran tests. I was told David had severe allergies and asthmatic conditions. The doctor opened a large medical book in his office and showed me hideous pictures of what my son would endure in the months and years ahead. He declared there was no cure!

Leaving the military hospital to head home, I secured David into his car seat and began to pray. I was given Luke 18:27 which reads, "But He said, What is impossible with men is possible with God." (Luke 18:27) I felt the Lord close to me as I drove to our local church instead of going home. No one else was there as I opened the door, turned on the lights and took David in my arms to the altar in the sanctuary. I stood in the exact spot where he had been dedicated to the Lord when he was one month old. I lifted David to God and prayed a simple prayer, reminding the Lord that He had promised me a totally healthy baby boy. As we left the church, I knew in my heart there had been a transaction of faith. I recorded in my Bible eight months later that David's skin was totally normal. The whelps on his flesh disappeared over the months and they have never returned. Like Hannah, we went our way in peace with thanksgiving, for the God of Israel had answered our request.

A heart of prayer in alignment with God's heart can bring us to rare moments of divine connectivity and opportunity. So it was for Elizabeth, who had waited through long years of barrenness for her prayers to be answered. She and her husband Zachariah had earnestly sought the Lord for a child. Now that they were elderly, both of them had resigned themselves to their situation and felt their earlier hopes would never be fulfilled. But one appointed day, as Zachariah served in the altar at the temple, he had a sudden visitation from Heaven which changed their lives forever. An angel of the Lord appeared and told Zachariah a special child would be born and he gave specific instructions for the care of this baby boy, who was to be named John. Years of prayer would now come to a magnificent crescendo, break the reproach of barrenness, release a prophetic voice to stir a nation to repentance and usher in Jesus Christ.

Before the birth of John, the angel Gabriel came to make an announcement to a young woman named Mary. To her amazement, she was told she would become pregnant by the overshadowing of the Holy Spirit and her baby boy would be called Jesus. She believed the message and received the announcement in faith declaring, "Behold, I am the handmaiden of the Lord; let it be done to me according to what you have said. And the angel left her."(Luke 1:26-38) As Mary faced the hardships of her pregnancy and the responsibilities of raising Jesus, we can only imagine the times she sought God the Father for direction, strength and comfort.

After the birth of Jesus, we find an elderly prophetess of God named Anna in the temple waiting for the coming Messiah. She worshipped the Lord day and night with fasting and prayer. One day she was led by the Spirit to encounter Joseph, Mary and the infant Jesus when He was brought to Jerusalem to be dedicated to the Lord. Anna came into the court of the temple praising the Lord and declaring this child to be God's Redeemer. (Luke 2:37,38) We can only speculate how much her continuous fasting and praying had helped to protect Mary and the coming of the Lord.

At the age of 33, Jesus launched His ministry and began to be known in the land. We can be sure that during those three years, Mary pondered and prayed over many things in her own heart. When she asked for Jesus's assistance at the wedding in Cana, she revealed to the servants what she knew to be true as she instructed them, "Whatever He says to you, do it." (John 2:5) I would suggest those are still good words to live by.

Other handmaidens have also believed these words to be true, like the desperate Canaanite mother with the demon possessed daughter. She refused to be quieted as she persevered in her loud crying out to the

Lord for His intervention. The disciples could not silence her. Neither did the Lord's seeming rebuff stop her from continuing to cry out for her daughter's deliverance. She came and knelt at His feet, worshiping Him and praying, "Lord help me!"

Jesus replied to her, "It is not proper to give you the children's bread."

But in faith she said, "just give me a crumb," because she believed that just a crumb from His table was enough to heal and deliver her child! Jesus commended her great faith and from that moment her daughter was free. (Matthew 15:22-28)

After Christ's death and resurrection, we find his mother Mary worshiping and praying with the 120 in the upper room until they all received the outpouring of the Holy Spirit on the day of Pentecost. (Acts 1:14) Through earnest prayer, the Holy Spirit Who had once overshadowed her to conceive the Christ now filled her being with His Presence and power. What a tangible comfort that must have been to the Lord's handmaiden!

The church was birthed in the powerful demonstration of the Spirit and three thousand souls received the Lord as Savior through Peter's first sermon. As the church grew and was edified, many women joined in the new work contributing their faith, prayer, worship and service to God. Down through the generations it has continued to be so. How about us? Are we gazing, watching and waiting for the Lord in order to serve Him, be with Him, heed His voice and go at His command?

Years ago we were stationed at Ramstein, AFB Germany. We attended a protestant service held in a small military chapel on an Army Post near our village. We decided to hold a prayer breakfast for the ladies of the chapel. Our guest speaker was to be the Catholic priest, but that morning as we gathered to eat, he had not arrived. We were puzzled, but as time went by we became concerned. When we made the decision to walk into the sanctuary to pray, the chaplain came bursting in with apologies to everyone in the gathering. Then he began to share his testimony of why he was late.

He had a small dog which had been with him for many years. The night before our breakfast he arrived home from work but, instead of being greeted, there was blood on the floor and his dog was very still. He bundled up his pet and took the dog to a local veterinarian. He was not given much hope, but the doctor said he would call in the morning. He went home and prayed a long time for his pet of many years.

He shared with us that he began to think about the journey they had shared together. His dog would sleep at the foot of his bed every night and at the slightest motion or sound he would be up to guard his master. The first thing in the morning, the dog would follow him all over the house. He would greet him at the door when he came home from work.

The priest turned to us at that moment, moved with emotion, and said how good it would be if we were as faithful to watch for the Lord and serve Him as the dog had been to help his master. He had prayed most of the night. He apologized for not having a prepared message for the prayer breakfast, but we assured him that we felt we had heard a message directly from the heart of the Lord.

We started making our way to the altar to have a time of group prayer, when suddenly the secretary of the chapel office came into the room announcing the veterinarian had just called. The doctor did not know how it was possible, but the priest's little dog lived through the night and was able to come home. As the priest hastened to leave, we went into praising and thanking the Lord for His mercy. We had learned some penetrating truth during the prayer breakfast, which would be good to ponder again. Are we watching and serving the Lord with faithfulness? Are we guarding the work of the Kingdom through our prayers?

We find these words in Psalm 123:2, "Behold, as the eyes of servants look to the hand of their master, and as the eyes of a maid to the hand of her mistress, so our eyes look to the Lord our God, until He has mercy and loving-kindness for us." (Psalm 123:2) Do we need to carefully consider who and what has our riveted attention? The old statement that we become a reflection of what we gaze upon is true. May we set the right vision before us and make it plain.

Consider that thought and look at some of the handmaidens again: Eve as she gazed upon forbidden fruit; Miriam who watched over her tiny brother Moses as he floated on the Nile; Ruth as she watched Naomi and refused to leave her side; Deborah as she watched the generals of Israel win their battles; Hannah who watched in fervent prayer and looked to the Lord for a son; Esther who looked to God for the strategy to save her nation; and we have Mary, who gazed upon the angel Gabriel and believed God's plan. Later, she looked upon the Cross and became a follower of Christ and was filled with the Holy Spirit at Pentecost. These handmaidens directed their eyes and their hearts to receive from God for their generation. Can we not do the same?

Please join with me in prayer:

Lord God, we are grateful for the testimony of the faithfulness of these handmaidens who have gone before us. We are encouraged by their perseverance and freshly determine to be more diligent in seeking You. Forgive us for failing to come to You quickly for our every need. We ask for communion with You, our petitions to be answered by You and our intercession to be strong before You on behalf of others. We pray that the testimonies of Your handmaidens and their faithfulness to believe Your Word would enrich many more lives. We ask that we would also have a personal testimony to enlarge the faith of others and rejoice the hearts of many. We ask for Your Hand to rest upon Your handmaidens and servants all over the earth. Strengthen, equip, anoint and bless these men and women of God. In Jesus's name, Amen.

Considerations:

1. We see through these testimonies that women were used in marvelous ways to strengthen their generation and bring glory to the Lord Who answered their prayers. This is also happening today as women of courage persevere in earnest prayer and take their anointed positions in society. I encourage you to be steadfast and abound in the work of the Lord.

2. I believe Proverbs 31 demonstrates the balanced, powerful life of a virtuous praying woman capably running her home, honoring her husband and preparing for future days while engaged in business ventures. Please read it again soon. I am convinced the Lord still needs and counts upon His inspired, interceding handmaidens. Women have a very significant position in the Kingdom of God, which begins and is maintained at their private altar. Let us seek Him in this hour of grace and remember the words of Mary at the marriage of Cana, "Whatever He says to you—Do it." **(John 2:5)**

Notes

Notes

Chapter 11 — The Altars of Jesus Christ

Philippians 2:8

And after He had appeared in human form, He abased and humbled Himself
[still further] and carried His obedience to the extreme of death,
even the death of the cross.

Over the past ten chapters, we have considered altars of various kinds and descriptions. We have seen that an altar is an integral part of mankind's need to have a definite place to worship and experience God. In his book *Things We Adore,* Judson Cornwall states that, "Few of us successfully pour out our adoration to an abstract concept."[16] Therefore, I suggest that a tangible altar which we can see, touch and revisit actually becomes a holy place, helping us to fellowship in worship and prayer with God and release our faith for definite answers from our heavenly Father. This is not merely the maintenance of a religious rite, but the potential increase of our awareness of the Lord and the expansion of a growing, vital relationship with Him. In our chosen sanctuary, our spirit connects with the Holy Spirit, releasing us into an awareness of God's Presence. Conversely, the Lord has found a place to rest and is at home in us! We must never forget we have been invited to know and experience the King in the now of our lives! I implore you to seize the opportunity to know Him in deeper ways. He longs for us to come and seek Him.

I have personally witnessed that altars can have a great impact! I invite you to go back for a moment in your own thoughts and consider altars you have seen or perhaps even had the privilege to stand or kneel to actively participate in worship. Then come and take a brief journey with me as I remember and point out a few of my altar experiences and the revelations of Christ which have come to me along the way.

—There was a simple, carved-out place forming a communion table in the solid rock of a large cave hidden in the mountain side overlooking Salzburg, Austria. Here at this altar, the local body of believers had met secretly when their lives were endangered..

—There was a small table covered in hand-crocheted lace in Jebel, Bulgaria, where a handful of worshippers gathered in an old building and cried out to the Lord for His mercy and grace to come to that dusty Muslim village near the Turkish/Greek border.

—Across Italy, there was cathedral after cathedral leading pilgrims all the way to Rome and the magnificence of St. Peter's Cathedral and the Vatican. But the cathedral I remember with real joy was in Florence. We has been touring Italy and walked into this huge edifice. We looked at the beautiful artistry, mosaics with vivid scenes depicted from the scriptures, but my young son David got my full attention when he

---

[16] Things We Adore, Judson Cornwall, P. 5

quietly declared, "Mom, Jesus is here." I instantly stopped looking at the brilliant art work and paid attention to the Spirit. When I shifted my focus from the temporal to the eternal, I began to hear the worship and my eyes turned to a far corner of the great cathedral, where a small group of followers were worshipping by a magnificent golden altar. Their praise had ushered in His Presence and I had the privilege of being touched by their love and His.

—On a sunny day, we walked about a mile through a dense forest near the Rhine River in Germany and came upon a hidden castle. When we toured the inside, we found there was an altar on the top floor in the master bedroom with a carved table and beautiful stain glass windows. We were told they had wanted God's blessings and built their altar as close to Heaven as possible.

—In recent years, I have repeatedly visited the small chapel on the YWAM Base grounds in Garden City, Texas. Here, these dedicated young people have unique altars where you can study, create a prophetic drawing, play an instrument or pray for the nations. I love to go visit that chapel just to join with them and pray with anyone who desires to touch Jesus. Every individual has a story to tell of God's mercy and grace in bringing them to this place of training, which prepares them to be launched into the mission fields of the world.

—In the years of ministry and many associations around the world, I have rejoiced over *coffee table* altars in living rooms. Then there were the wonderful meals of fellowship served in dining rooms, as we broke bread together and shared our journey in Christ. These are moments of heart-to-heart relationship and I truly believe the Lord is present and takes pleasure in the conversations of the brethren. After all, did He not *sup* with His disciples after His Resurrection?

The validity, authority and fresh anointing released through altars of true prayer is an effervescent inspiration to me. It bubbles up, overflows and speaks Life into my soul. Whenever I travel across America or to distant lands, my suitcase holds an altar in a *portable form*. I pack my prayer shawl, Bible, atlas, prayer pages, anointing oil and daily journal. Whatever my destination, as soon as I am established where I will rest for the night; I anoint the room with prayer and declare the blessings of the Lord over my temporary space. I lay hands on the bed, declaring God's peace, and cleanse the room of anything that has happened there which was not of the Lord. I touch every window and door and declare the enemy has no access. The Holy Spirit always guides these prayers in specific ways according to what has happened or what could happen in that room. I thank God for the authority we have been given. I welcome the Holy Spirit and the angels of God into my new space to abide in the room with me. I place my prayer shawl on the bed with my Bible and journal close by. There is peace for I have established Holy ground!

This is the way that I possess the room for Kingdom purposes and it grants me serenity no matter what the neighborhood; and believe me, sometimes it has been "the hood"! I have often thanked God that I did not know where I was until the dawn of the new day, when in the daylight I looked outside and saw the difficulties of my location. Truly He has been and He ever shall be my Keeper!

I remember when we went to Northern India and traveled to Darjeeling to minister in a local church, I was ushered into a nice second story room of a hotel overlooking the city. I was given total privacy in order to prepare for the services. This downtown hotel was resting in the midst of a *spiritual triangle* containing a Mosque, a Hindu temple and a Buddhist temple. Hmmmm…trust me when I say their faithfulness to worship began very early every morning. The first night, I asked the Lord how I was to get any rest in this room and I was instructed to get into the bed, cover my blankets with my prayer shawl and go to sleep in perfect peace. Every morning while we were there, I was awakened by the Lord at exactly four o'clock to pray and study until seven. The nights were chilly and I was grateful that coffee arrived at my door at six o'clock! During this stay, despite all the noise in the streets and the oppressive atmosphere, I was at total peace; plus, I had perfect clarity in my study time and anointing to share the Word in the services. This was the covering of God through prayer and obedience.

Altars, even *portable altars*, release a presence of the Lord and a covering of His Wings. Please read Psalm 91 and Psalm 121 in connection with my testimony. An additional notation and insight into this story is that several of the team members in Darjeeling told me later that the Lord instructed them to pray for me during these hours. Amen. How grateful we are for the unified support of such intercessory prayer.

In our study of altars, we have considered altars made of mounds of dirt, uncut stone, wood covered with polished brass or ornate gold. These altars have helped individuals and even nations bridge the gap between Earth and Heaven; flesh and Spirit. As we worship the Lord, an altar should be a place of ever-increasing revelation.

However, it is the worshipper and the God he is worshipping that have made these various altars places of genuine encounter with Deity. A human heart is never satisfied until that Holy connection with the Living God is established by faith. In considering these things, I believe we must look to the blood-stained Cross of Calvary as the highest and most important altar for time and eternity. It is the blood Jesus surrendered and sacrificed on the Cross which saves, heals and delivers us. Hallelujah!

When I was a student in sixth grade in a small southern town, we actually had daily morning devotions. There were times my teacher would lead our class in the hymn *The Old Rugged Cross*. The verses of that song would touch my heart, even though at that time, I had not yet heard the plan of salvation. The Lord has His own way of speaking to each heart, and the anointed words in that old hymn spoke to me and created a hunger to know Jesus.

In this chapter, I want us to share portions of the Gospels prior to the Cross and observe some places where Jesus communed with and worshiped the Father. We know that even at the early age of twelve, He mystified the rabbis in the court of the temple at Jerusalem as He expounded on the Word of God and answered their questions. (Luke 2:46) This causes me to understand Jesus was already in close prayer and fellowship with His Father. However, we only have insights into His Life and not a biography. The last verse of John's Gospel declares, "*And there are also many other things which Jesus did. If they should be all recorded one by one [in detail], I suppose that even the world itself could not contain (have room for) the books that would be written.*" (John 21:25)

In Luke 18:1, Jesus told His disciples to be constant and persevering in prayer, "*Also [Jesus] told them a parable to the effect that they ought always to pray and not to turn coward (faint, lose heart, and give up).*" In order to have such victory in prayer, a believer has to go beyond a few petitions, a brief touch of comfort or sudden cries for help in an hour of need. Prayer or conversing with God must become a way of life, a flowing stream of our constantly yielding to the Holy Spirit and receiving what only He can give to us. This constant provision for us is why the Holy Spirit came and why He has stayed! He is our daily Helper and Paraclete! I am convinced that prayer is like muscle tissue and must be daily exercised and used.

In studying the word I in the Greek, we find it means to implore, beseech, seek, ask, desire, petition, pray earnestly, supplicate, worship or make a request. These are verbs describing active communication with

God and the scripture says that out of the abundance of our heart we speak. (Luke 6:45) True prayer is a language of the heart. It is an amazing, life-giving relationship with God Himself. Out of our close association with Him, vibrant prayer becomes a two-way conversation. If this is not true for you, I invite you to draw closer and deepen your fellowship with the Holy Spirit. We have a promise that He prays through us!!! Let's look at Romans 8:27, "*And He Who searches the hearts of men knows what is in the mind of the [Holy] Spirit [what His intent is], because the Spirit intercedes and pleads [before God] in behalf of the saints according to and in harmony with God's will.*"

Many people feel they cannot pray properly and therefore they hesitate to even try. There is actual fear attached to such a statement. We can never fail to speak what is right when we are expressing our hearts to a loving Father. His arms and His heart are opened wide to us and He will never reject us.

He gave instruction to His disciples, "*But when you pray, go into your [most] private room, and, closing the door, pray to your Father, Who is in secret; and your Father, Who sees in secret, will reward you in the open.*" (Matthew 6:6) This passage of scripture strongly supports the concept of having your own private altar or a designated place that you have set aside where you meet with God on a regular basis. Why is this necessary? Can't we just run and pray at the same time? You can and you can't. Prayer is always possible. There are times it can simply be a continuous flow of conversation between you and the Lord. But focused prayer, prayer with a goal in mind, prayer concerning definite needs or battles which must be won, prayer that needs an answer in order to take action must be wrought in a place of solitude with no distractions in order to focus your total attention on the Lord. This means no electronic equipment is allowed! In this place of privacy there must be the liberty to freely express out loud the longings of your heart, your personal opinions and not be concerned with time or people.

Many people do not pray because they are intimidated by the possible opinions of those around them. So I encourage you again to get alone with God on a regular basis and, in that set-apart place, take time to listen and hear His voice. Ask Him to teach you how to pray. The disciples asked to be taught! Allow your prayer time to become a two-way conversation in which you find out who you are in Him and who you are becoming by His grace. Prayer brings forth transformation, because we are made alive in God.

Chiseling definite time out of our busy daily schedule to spend those minutes focused only on the Lord because we love Him becomes a fueling station to energize and maintain our walk with Christ. Every believer needs a private place of Divine encounter. No one else could possibly grant us the wisdom, knowledge, companionship, strength, comfort and victory communicated through the Holy Spirit. Embrace Him as your best Friend!

When I began to maintain a daily walk with Christ, my life was completely changed. I am convinced that what we worship is what we become. Being steadfast in our worship of the Lord keeps a steady flow of the Spirit in our veins. Let us remember the words of Jesus in John 15:5, "*I am the Vine; you are the branches. Whoever lives in Me and I in him bears much (abundant) fruit. However, apart from Me [cut off from vital union with Me] you can do nothing.*"

I have learned my intercession is not measured by the amount of time, but rather the way I am led by the Holy Spirit during those daily encounters that changes me and releases me to become more. He is alive! Life was meant to be lived energized by the God Who created us. I am convinced that life, especially in the western world, has become too busy, too loud and too multi-tasked. We are so scattered and stretched we find it difficult to focus or even grasp private moments of genuine solitude. We look good and sound good but our spiritual tanks are on empty!

The majority of people work their eight-hour shifts, drive defensively through traffic to get home, walk into their house after a busy day and do not even take one breathe of peace to detox from the pressures of the day, but instead go straight to turn-on switches and fill the sanctuary of their home with more distraction and noise. I think we need to prayerfully reprogram ourselves!

According to the scriptures, Jesus prayed in different locations such as the mountains, the hills or a grove of olive trees. He would often withdraw from active ministry to be alone with His Heavenly Father. *"And after He had taken leave of them, He went off into the hills to pray."* (Mark 6:48) He sought the Presence of His Father and knew He had to hear His Voice and experience His Love. Many times the only way this was possible was to pray during the night hours, when the people and His disciples were asleep.

Jesus would also take certain ones of His disciples with Him to pray. On one such occasion, He took Peter, John and James to the top of a mountain. When He began to pray, the disciples fell asleep and when they awakened, their eyes beheld the glory of God upon Jesus's countenance and even His clothing was dazzling with Light and flashing like lightening. A cloud came and encompassed them and out of the cloud the Father spoke and declared, "This is My Son, My Chosen One or My Beloved; listen to and yield to and obey Him!" (Luke 9:35)

As the disciples walked with Christ, they would have opportunity to listen to Jesus pray to the Father. One day, they requested He would teach them how to communicate with God the Father as He did. Out of that prayer pattern found in Luke 11, we see the need to honor God, desire His Kingdom to be established in the Earth, ask for daily provision, live in a spirit of forgiveness and guard ourselves against temptation. At this time, the Lord also gave them a teaching on pressing on, persevering in prayer and daring to believe that God will definitely answer our cries to Him.

I know when I have been burdened or deeply concerned over personal situations or the needs of ministry, the Holy Spirit has often guided me to the Gospel of John and I have read chapters 14-21 again and again. This section of the Gospels has always set me in fresh alignment and steadied my walk. For I cannot observe the cost Jesus paid at the Cross without being changed.

During the hours just prior to His crucifixion, Jesus shared and demonstrated many teachings and exhortations with His disciples. (John 14-16) On that long ago night, that Passover table became an altar as the Lamb of God prepared to be our sacrifice. It is written that Jesus lifted His eyes to His Father and prayed the most incredible prayer for each of us. He sanctified Himself so that we might be sanctified. His plea was to bring glory and honor to His Father. His desire was to give eternal life to all who would ever believe on Him. He defined it for us, *"And this is eternal life: [it means] to know (to perceive, recognize, become acquainted with, and understand) You, the only true and real God, and [likewise] to know Him, Jesus [as the] Christ (the Anointed One, the Messiah), Whom You have sent."* (John 17:3) I say amen and may His glory be achieved in our lives.

Leaving that table, they went out into the dark streets of Jerusalem and made their way through the city gate and across the waters of the Kidron to the Garden of Gethsemane. Arriving in this secluded place, the disciples were instructed to watch and pray, but they promptly fell asleep. The scripture does not say that Jesus knelt over a big rock, as we have often pictured. It is written that Jesus began to deeply sorrow and threw Himself to the ground as He agonized in prayer for the souls of men. Luke 22:44 states, "*And being in an agony [of mind], He prayed [all the] more earnestly and intently, and His sweat became like great clots of blood dropping down upon the ground.*" The dirt of the Earth became the first receiver of His Sacrifice. The disciples slept while an angel came from Heaven to strengthen the Lord in His hour of need.

Jesus was arrested and forcefully taken through a mockery of a trial, suffered unjust treatment, the scorn of men, a fierce whipping by the Roman soldiers and then was nailed to the Cross. Hanging between Heaven and Earth as His life blood streamed out of His body, He forgave those who caused Him such agony, gave His mother to John's care and gave His life into the hand of the Father. On this cruel altar, the price of salvation was fully paid for all time. It was finished!

There has never been a more expressive altar of Divine communication than the Cross of Calvary. When we understand the agonizing price Jesus paid for mankind to be saved and receive that sacrifice personally into our own hearts, then the sign of the Cross will always stir our hearts to humility, love, worship and devotion.

Please join with me in prayer:

Father God, we approach your throne with humility and love. We thank you for the shed blood of Your Son which frees us from all sin and prepares us for all blessings. If anyone reading these pages has not yet accepted Christ as their Savior, we ask for their Salvation. We declare our need of a Savior and we receive forgiveness through His blood sacrifice. We ask for strength to follow on to know the Lord in Spirit and in Truth. Help us to take daily time to worship, learn and pray. May the Holy Spirit use us to share the Good News of the Gospel with all we meet. In Jesus's Name, Amen.

Considerations:

1. As you have read this chapter, perhaps altars have stood out in a new way. For a moment, think about encounters with God you have received at an altar. Thank Him with a grateful heart. Let's believe for more of His presence which leads us into His glory!

2. I am convinced that the average church, especially in America, creates a good deal of rhetoric and many programs which illuminate the minds of believers, yet do not promote and establish deep personal relationship in the Holy Spirit. When we really encounter God Himself at a heart level, we are forever ruined for anything less than the magnificent friendship of God through the work of His Spirit. Therefore, I ask that we consider the measure of our loyalty to Jesus Christ Himself! Do we know Him or just about Him? Do we follow Him or just ask Him to bless our plans?

3. Do we, like the disciples, need to ask the Lord to teach us how to pray? How do we communicate in true dialogue with Him? I think the greatest key is to learn how to come and wait upon Him. Our devotion is not a 5-minute daily morning reading with a brief written prayer. Devotion means set-aside time, interaction with the Lord, passion and focused vision. Let Him capture your heart!

Notes

Chapter 12 — The Altars of His Church

1 Peter 2:24

He personally bore our sins in His [own] body on the tree [as on an altar
and offered Himself on it], that we might die (cease to exist) to sin
and live to righteousness. By His wounds you have been healed.

I welcome you to this 12th chapter of *Come and Dine with the King* with an expectant heart, for I believe the Lord will speak to us in a special way and grant fresh vision of His earnest call to prayer. I ask for the Spirit of the Lord to stir our imagination, creating vivid insights and stimulate within us His Divine purposes for our lives. It is vital to use our imagination when we pray, read God's Word or come to Him in worship. Can we dare to believe for greater things, lift up our countenance to Him and allow the Lord to open our eyes to see and comprehend a broader picture? It is my prayer for us, as God's children, to have the eyes of our hearts enlightened by the anointing of the Holy Spirit, releasing fresh images of His glorious plans for every life. Jesus is alive and we have been made alive in Him.

As we enter this chapter, let me ask you a few questions: What have you seen in Heaven? What is your image of God's throne? Have you heard God laugh? Have you seen the tears of concern rolling down your Savior's face? Have you felt the pressure of His grip as He reached for your hand, the hand of a friend? Have you witnessed the King fully dressed for battle? Have you felt His Presence during worship as His great wings encompassed and secured your soul? He is the Risen Lord and He is vibrantly with us this very hour. I ask Jesus to open our eyes, our ears and hearts to know and experience Him.

In the previous chapter, we focused on the absolutely highest altar for time and eternity — the Lord laying down His Life on the Cross of Calvary for the salvation of all who would ever believe on Him. I cannot visualize His sacrifice without humbling myself in thanksgiving before Him. Beyond words to express, Jesus Christ is worthy of our worship and adoration. We know that after His death and burial the grave could not hold Him, and on the third day He arose from the dead. Now that is a reality check and a powerful picture that needs to be painted on our hearts forever! In fact, when I have difficulties and need strength to continue the journey, I read from John 14-21. I focus once again on the liberty He has given and the price He paid for me. Hallelujah! This freedom is for all who will believe! Thank you, Jesus!

In the last verses of the book of Luke, the resurrected Christ walks up and joins two of His despondent followers who are walking on the road to Emmaus. He questions them about their heavy discussion and they begin to declare their feelings of despair and loss. They continue to walk and express their difficult questions of *what now*? The Lord seizes the opportunity to expound the Word of God to them and explains the scriptural necessity of His sacrifice.

In the early evening, they came to a place of rest and they convinced Christ to enter and partake of a meal with them. Sitting together at a table, Jesus took a loaf of bread, praised God and gave thanks. As He gave them their portion, their eyes were opened to truly recognize the Risen Lord in their midst. Jesus then vanished from their presence. Without hesitation, they arose right then and went with haste to Jerusalem to tell the disciples they had seen the Lord. (Luke 24:13-32)

Beloved, if we look, we shall see. If we gaze, we shall come to greater understanding. If we listen, we shall hear His voice of instruction. Like these disciples so long ago may our eyes be opened, for the Christ is often in our midst!

I still remember one of the first times I encountered the tangible presence of the Lord in a church service, when I was touched by the Holy Spirit during the preaching. Following the message, the pastor gave an altar call; I hastened to reach the railing and knelt before the Lord. The pastor's wife came over and earnestly prayed with me. In that moment of seeking God, it seemed like all the burdens of life melted away and I experienced a pure white glory enveloping my whole being. My eyes were closed, but I could see I was totally immersed in pure, white light. In that moment of time, nothing mattered but the depth of His peace and presence.

No words could fully express this encounter, but I can still visualize and feel the spiritual transaction which took place. Just as the Lord made Himself tangibly real to the disciples long ago, He revealed the reality of Himself to me, while I was a brand new, baby Christian. The revelation of His presence has grown and matured over the years. I have continued to deeply rejoice in what I call *encounters of the Highest Kind*. Yet today, I am challenged to look and to seek again, for there is so much more to know and experience. Life was meant to be lived vibrantly, not tolerated and endured. We have often used the phrase, "Wake up and smell the coffee!" May the dawning of each new day find us quickened by the Spirit and drinking deeply of His steadfast love.

When the disciples reached Jerusalem and met with the others, they shared all that had happened on the road. While they testified of these things, the Lord startled them by appearing in their midst. Joy and excitement filled the house, as He shared the scriptures, ate with them and encouraged them to remain in Jerusalem and seek the Father for the outpouring of the Holy Spirit. (Luke 24:49)

Luke continues his writings about these events after the Resurrection in the Book of Acts. Following the Lord's ascension to Heaven, we find the first altar for the followers of Christ was in the upper room, where 120 waited for the promised Holy Spirit with steadfast, unified prayer believing that the promise of the Lord would be fulfilled. They were not disappointed, for on the day of Pentecost the Holy Spirit came like a mighty, loud wind from Heaven filling their upper room as tongues of fire came upon every believer present. These scriptures declare that this powerful presence of the Spirit brought forth different languages with clear and loud expression. (Acts 2:4)

This outpouring was demonstrated to the city as many people heard the great wind and wondered what was taking place. They gathered around the disciples and questioned how the languages of their nations were being brought forth by uneducated people. This set the stage for Peter to boldly preach the Good News, and the anointing upon him ushered in 3,000 new believers in one day. (Acts 2:41) In the months afterwards, there were signs, wonders, instruction and fellowship as the church grew and the Lord daily added souls to their number. In the midst of the continuing prayers and growth of the church, there were also persecutions, hardships, imprisonments and directives from the Lord to go to the ends of the Earth with the Gospel. Their altars of prayer created a *launching pad* for the salvation of souls and the demonstrations of God's love and power to the nations.

In those days, the apostle Peter was in Joppa and the roof of the house where he was staying became an altar before the Lord. Peter was stunned and caught off guard by the command of the Lord that day. But as he continued to gaze on the vision of the *unclean things*, he submitted to the command of the Lord and went with the support of witnesses to the house of Cornelius. When he began to share the truth of the Gospel, He was amazed at the great outpouring of the Holy Spirit upon a household of Gentile believers. No one could deny it was the work of God.

We are in a season of great change and the need for active obedience to the instructions of the Holy Spirit. There is a definite call in the Spirit to come closer to the Lord and diligently study the Word. It is easy to think we remember what the Word says, yet when we reread it, we find something new and pertinent to our lives. The Lord has taught me to be an active student of the Word. He will talk to us individually from the pages of Holy Scripture.

We live in a day when everyone wants a word from a "prophet." I am anointed and available to the Lord to give words of encouragement and exhortation to many; whether it happens over phone calls, emails, or in person, I do prophesy! But there is a great necessity for every believer to hear directly from the Lord for themselves, know His voice and live in a trusting relationship with God. The Holy Spirit has been given to guide and counsel all of us. He is our faithful Teacher and constant Companion. We must learn how to get still, hear and heed His Voice in the inner man. Jesus promised we would definitely hear Him, but we must quiet our thoughts and come to a level of peace to hear His voice.

Shortly after Peter visited Cornelius, Herod rose up and took violent action against leaders in the church. James was killed and Peter was taken captive. Many prayers rose to Heaven on behalf of Peter's life while he was chained in prison, and the Lord answered their cry. Suddenly, an angel of the Lord visited Peter and brought him out the gates of the prison. This magnificent testimony of Peter's deliverance has always made me smile, because Peter thought at first it was only a dream. When he arrived at the house where everyone had established an altar of prayer, he knocked excitedly on the entry door. However, he was left standing on the front porch when the young lady named Rhoda came to the door because she thought Peter was a ghost. It took a while to recognize that their fervent prayers had been dramatically answered.

The early church prayed and God brought deliverance from the persecution of Saul. But the Lord wanted to do more than stop Saul; He wanted Saul's heart changed. Through a dramatic conversion, Saul was knocked off of his *high horse* onto the sandy road of Damascus. The Lord revealed Himself to Saul and sealed his eyes so that he had to be led into the city. In a matter of days, his bed became his altar and he was converted by an obedient Ananias; Saul's name and his life were forever changed. He became a new creation renamed Paul and was mightily used by God to usher in the Gentiles.

Paul diligently traveled the known world and prayers were raised to God on his behalf while he boldly preached Christ. He waited for long periods in jail, and received the anointing of the Holy Spirit to write the letters to the churches (which became most of the New Testament). Intercession delivered Paul from whippings, beatings, false arrests, shipwreck and the bite of a venomous snake. The early church understood that fervent prayer in the name of Jesus released the power of God into the Earth to build His house and deliver souls from the oppression of the enemy.

This is still the powerful truth of the Gospel. Unified believers with hungry hearts and an active prayer life can usher in the dynamic works of the Holy Spirit. The Lord has not changed His mind, beloved; He is waiting for His people to believe, live for Him and activate His Word by faith. James 4:8 states, "Come close to God and He will come close to you..."

Altars release greater faith and bring us closer to the Lord's presence. Altars are mentioned 338 times in the scriptures. *They really are important*, even in this day of electronic devices and fast-paced schedules. When we read the New Testament and compare it to the church in this hour, we realize our need to pray for renewal, revival and restoration in the house of God.

I am convinced the key to breakthrough is fourfold: private plus corporate prayer, devotion to God and our quick obedience to the Holy Spirit. For me, these things were birthed and maintained in my life through a hunger to know God, continuing study of His Word, and faithfulness in my allegiance to Him. These things are maintained and increased by close personal relationship in my private daily altar before the Lord. This is my position of sight and hearing in the Spirit. My prayer is that He will ever increase and I will decrease.

I was recently in a southwestern city and had the opportunity to minister to a young lady who was in great pain because of a sexually transmitted disease. She had been abused from an early age and then made some wrong decisions that added to her difficulties in her teenage years. However, like the woman at the well, she was hungry to know the Lord in Spirit and in truth. In that meeting, the love of God poured out upon her and she was filled with the Holy Spirit. After the washing of many tears, she looked deeply into my eyes and said, "I have never seen Jesus before, but I see Him in you." That holy moment of prayer connection in His loving Presence brought help and hope to her broken, fragmented life. We live in a damaged world, but we serve a healing Jesus!

One of my favorite pictures of Jesus in the scriptures, upon which I often gaze, is found in Revelation 1. No longer is He on the Cross — He is risen indeed! He is King of all Kings and Lord of all Lords. As we behold Him in these verses of scripture, He is absolutely breathtaking in His glory and power! Like John, the Beloved, all we can do is bow and worship.

Revelation 1: 12-16

"Then I turned to see [whose was] the voice that was speaking to me, and on turning I saw seven golden lampstands,

And in the midst of the lampstands [One] like a Son of Man, clothed with a robe which reached to His feet and with a girdle of gold about His breast.

His head and His hair were white like white wool, [as white] as snow, and His eyes [flashed] like a flame of fire.

His feet glowed like burnished (bright) bronze as it is refined in a furnace, and His voice was like the sound of many waters.

In His right hand He held seven stars, and from His mouth there came forth a sharp two-edged sword, and His face was like the sun shining in full power at midday."

Quite often I hear people say they want to see the Lord. I think He is very merciful in displaying Himself only to the level we can handle the revelation. It will be such an awesome day when, with our glorified bodies, we can truly behold Him in fullness. I anticipate that moment with great joy! But until He comes, let us be found faithful.

I have a small wooden cross which stands on my altar as a daily reminder. The vertical center beam speaks to me of reaching to God, drawing my strength from Him, realizing like Jacob of old there is a transaction taking place between Heaven and Earth. The horizontal beam reminds me of the necessity of ministering such love to others not merely with words, but with deeds of kindness. There are many ways we can express the Lord daily through individual lives. The world around us desperately needs the Living Jesus.

Recently when we held an Eagles meeting, a small group of us went out to fellowship after the gathering. It had become rather late, but we finally found a taco place that was still open. We ordered our food and had some good fellowship. As it was time to leave the restaurant, one of our ladies was stopped by a waitress and had the opportunity to share with her that we were late in coming to eat, because we had been in a church meeting. The young waitress immediately replied. "You were in church? You are having a joyful time. Could you please pray for me?" That late night taco table became an altar of His grace, as she wept her way into the Kingdom of God. I felt as we headed home that this was a Divine encounter which we must expect to happen again and again; the Lord setting up sudden opportunities to save and comfort the lost. May we be bold to declare His Love to whomever we encounter.

In considering the altars of the scriptures throughout the pages of this book, I pray that I have been able to bring forth a new understanding and enlarged vision of the purpose of maintaining a personal altar. My great desire is to bring forth God's answers and the work of the Lord into the Earth. The Lord has chosen for each of us to live in a pivotal moment of time. May we seize every opportunity to proclaim the Good News and bring many more to His throne of grace. May the Lord bless you and lead you forward in His plans and purposes for your life.

Please join with me in prayer:

Father, we ask for eyes to see and ears to hear the things of the Spirit. We ask for greater faith and boldness to declare the things of God. Please show us how to make definite spiritual progress in our daily lives. We ask to be placed strategically into the position you have chosen for us in this season. May we be found faithful and bring glory to your matchless Name. From the purity of our hearts, we ask You to anoint our imaginations to perceive in the realm of the Spirit. Above all, Lord, may we bring You joy as we obey Your call and serve You to the ends of the Earth. In Jesus's Name, Amen.

Considerations:

1. What is the most important thing you know about Jesus Christ? How do you describe Him to other people? How do you convey your faith in a real world? Do you? Are you a witness of what you believe? After His Resurrection, Jesus told His disciples to *go*! Where? Into all the known world! This is an hour when the word *go* is written very large in those who are His disciples.

2. Although prayer is not about how many minutes we pray each day, it *is* about taking time for true association absorbing, exploring and drinking in the things of God. Prayer is alive and generates life! Prayer is your heart lifted in faith to God, knowing He is listening and answering! Ultimately, prayer is not about us, but about Him and the building of the Kingdom!

Notes

Notes

Chapter 13—Information to Help You Establish Your Altar

Joshua 22:26 ...

*So we said, Let us now prepare to **build** us an **altar...***

I have mentioned in these twelve chapters several ways the Lord has guided and strengthened my prayer altar through the years. My altar developed from a small table with a Bible and journal to a larger coffee table with a Bible, journal and prayer notebook full of photos, prayer requests and scriptures. Then I advanced to a prayer room of intercession holding the same materials surrounded by maps of the nations and vision for the Kingdom on all the walls.

My personal altar table holds a menorah, a shofar, communion elements, and a huge Bible. I also have my CD player, personal Bible, prayer shawl, devotional books, prayer notebook and a prayer journal close by. Start your altar with what seems suitable to you, then see how it works and build upon it as you continue to pray.

I am endeavoring to cast vision in this book to cause a stir in your heart to know that your prayer life can greatly increase plus your growing relationship with God deepen and become more satisfying. I sincerely request that you seek the Lord and ask Him how you can make your prayer time a real encounter, more alive and relational, and see definite answers to your prayers!

I encourage you to make one spot—your spot on Earth HOLY GROUND!

<u>Let me share some bullets of information for your consideration:</u>

1. A major need in prayer is our co-operation with the Holy Spirit. He knows how to pray effectively and His prayers are always correct. I try to listen, obey and just yield to His abilities!

2. I strongly encourage you to be filled with the Holy Spirit and allow Him Who is an ever-present help to pray through you. It is by doing that we learn to lean into His absolute guidance and counsel.

3. Let's get started. In the beginning steps of your prayer time, set aside the time that is best for you and works with your family. When my family was young, my 5 AM call worked very well. I usually prayed and shared with the Lord for an hour. My family needs started at 6 AM. On

weekends I could possibly take more time, but I always made Saturdays family time—Sundays were church time.

4. It is a necessity that you determine not to be hindered or interrupted. When you start this new pattern of seeking God, the enemy will try to divert your thoughts — the phone will ring, a text message will arrive, etc. If this is your time with God every day, seal it off in every way possible and have privacy to pray. As you do this day by day, you are truly establishing the Lord as first in your life and you will begin to experience greater sensitivity to the Holy Spirit.

5. Enter into these moments with reverence and expectation. As you come into the Lord's presence, spend time in worship from your heart. Each prayer time should be different, because the Holy Spirit is leading you. He makes this time rich and alive!

6. When you first enter this time, take a few moments to clear your thoughts. I take a memo pad and write down the order of my day. Life is always busy and I may need to run errands, write emails, make phone calls or keep an appointment. I list these things quickly and then I lay the pad aside. I will pick it up when my devotional time is finished.

7. During your prayer time, you may want to pray through some personal or family situations. The Spirit may remind you of other needs that friends or ministers have brought to your attention. These, too, can be lifted to God. There is nothing too small nor anything too big for God. Look through a microscope and then look through a telescope or God created it all and manages it well.

8. Write down in your journal any impressions or thoughts from the Lord. Don't just pray for others. What is on your heart? What is on His heart? Prayer is meant to be a dialogue, not a monologue.

9. As you draw near to the Lord, you will feel impressions. I suggest you follow the lead of the Holy Spirit. For instance, some mornings the Lord has me read more scripture than time in actual prayer. Other days I need to worship Him more and go deeper into His heart. This is not a religious duty, but an interchange from heart to heart. My response to the Holy Spirit keeps me in a flow of communication and creates a strong, satisfying relationship. He knows how to pray...I simply follow His lead.

15 Things that are really needed:

1. A commitment to seek Him

2. Faith

3. A listening ear—a hearing, humble heart

4. Spiritual sight and insight

5. Obedience to the Holy Spirit

6. An ever-growing knowledge of God's Word

7. A good scripture reference book to pray the Word over issues

8. Organization and preparedness

9. Prioritizing of current needs...what is number one?

10. Uninterrupted space

11. Focus and Concentration—yet be at ease

12. Be led—not driven

13. Find the best time of day for you...when are you alert?

14. Remember it's a dialogue—two coming together to mutually share

How do you create a Prayer Book?

First, go to an office supply store and purchase:

1. A 1inch binder or larger

2. A set of dividers to separate the prayer sections

3. Clear plastic cover sheets for your prayer needs or photos,etc.

4. A small plastic pouch to hold prayer request notes handed to you

5. A notebook-sized World Atlas or a globe to lay hands on the nations

6. A map of your region/state/nation. Begin with your local area/region —

   Because you have special authority to pray over your region.

More Vision Casting:

Please consider these possibilities and let them work for you!

1. You can use advertisement fliers for meetings, your church bulletin, business cards, photographs, emails, prayer lists, scriptures, etc. —

   Whatever will help to focus your attention and connect in your heart to bring forth definite prayer.

2. Gather all your information and photos to place them in the plastic covers. This protects them and allows you to lay hands on them.

   Faith is released at a higher level when we visualize and touch.

3. Mark your dividers into sections for prayer:

   Family—Workplace—-Ministry— Church—Lists of needs—

   Local region—- State—Nation—International

4. Add other sections to your prayer book for whatever you are concerned about.

   The dividers put the information right at your fingertips to turn and pray.

5. I use a map of the region and a phone directory to pray over the city.

   Every street, citizen, elected state representatives, school, hospital, church and far more have already been placed in categories for prayer.

6. Put in photos of your family, friends, ministries, etc.

   Add the scriptures you are praying over these people and ministries.

7. I use fliers or ads from ministries to pray over upcoming meetings.

8. I insert emails of prayer needs I have received.

9. I have scriptures I use to pray over governments and nations.

10. I go to the latest news reports and glean "bullets" for prayer.

11. I also use prayer materials and news provided by other ministries

12. There will be times the Lord has a strategic focus for your intercession.

    Turn to the prayer page He points out and go after it

Write down anything He shares and begin to pray in agreement with what He has revealed to you.

Organized this way, you can go around the world led by the Holy Spirit

in 30-45 minutes!

How pleasing such prayer is to the Father.

You have received an invitation...
Come and Dine with the King

Notes

Notes

CPSIA information can be obtained at www.ICGtesting.com
Printed in the USA
LVOW09s2234250614

391579LV00002B/3/P